SERBIAN DIARIES

To my friends Dragan, who translated my diaries into English, mon Poulet from Paris, my old Zita and the Princess Dragomirof who used to say: "My life is a sad story."

Serbian Diaries

Boris L. Davidovich

translated from the Serbo-Croat by
Dragan Vujanić

★★★

THE GAY MEN'S PRESS
LONDON

First published 1996 by GMP Publishers Ltd,
P O Box 247, London N6 4BW

British Library Cataloguing in Publication Data

Davidovich, Boris L.
Serbian diaries
1. Davidovich, Boris L. - Diaries 2. Gay men - Serbia - Belgrade - Diaries
I. Title
891.'285'03
ISBN 0854492224

Distributed in Europe by Central Books,
99 Wallis Rd, London E9 5LN

Distributed in North America by InBook, Division of LPC Group,
1436 West Randolph Street, Chicago, IL 60607

Distributed in Australia by Bulldog Books,
P O Box 155, Broadway, NSW 2007

Printed and bound in the EU by Norhaven A/S, Viborg, Denmark

I : 1986—1989
FREEDOM FROM COMMUNISM

II : 1991—1993
WAR AND DISASTER

I : 1986—1989
FREEDOM FROM COMMUNISM

June 3rd, 1986

The Army Hospital

Marko and I were still having a relationship at the time he got infected with hepatitis B. He probably caught it from someone he had sex with. I didn't get infected since I'd had hepatitis about five or six years earlier. I was sick for almost a year then and stayed more than half the time in bed.

Because Marko's father was a colonel he was sent to the Army Hospital. It was the best and most fashionable hospital in Belgrade, so staying there was a privilege reserved exclusively for the communist elite, the army, and those with good connections. When I was ill, I couldn't get to the Army Hospital but instead went into the old, damp, smelly Infectious Diseases Clinic built before the First World War.

Marko's bed was in the infectious diseases ward. You were only allowed to visit him if you stayed on the terrace outside the rooms. Patients and visitors had to talk through hermetically sealed windows using a phone system installed on both sides of the glass. The set-up reminded me of modern prisons. During the visit the space outside Marko's room was always crowded with his relatives so we never had the opportunity of talking openly or at length. I therefore decided to visit him one morning outside of visiting hours. I easily managed to jump over a low gate in front of the staircase and climbed up to the terrace.

Marko was alone in his room. His roommate, a married captain with two kids, was also a hepatitis patient. At the time he was out watching tv in the lounge. Marko approached the window, picked up the phone and began talking with me. We talked about all sorts of banal things, but we both felt rather horny because we hadn't had sex for ages — in fact since he went into hospital twenty days previously. We started saying sexy things to each other like, "I'd like to suck your prick right now", "I want to shove my dick into your arse so hard you scream", and so on. This sex over the phone and through the glass excited us so much that we both had hard-ons. I could see his cock completely erect beneath his pyjamas. I told him to take it out. He took his cock out and started jerking off, pressing it against the cold, smooth surface of the window from time to time. That turned me on so much I couldn't stand it any longer. I told him, wait a bit — I'm coming in to you!

It was difficult to enter the Army Hospital unofficially and especially the infectious diseases ward. Nevertheless, I used to visit a friend of mine there, a doctor who also worked at my faculty as a professor. We became friends and did various sorts of favours for each other. He worked at the Army Medical Institute, which was in the same building, but with a different entrance. I went to that entrance and told the soldier at the gate that I wanted to visit Dr Mišić. He phoned Dr Mišić who confirmed my visit. The soldier took my papers and gave me a pass which I hung on my collar. I told Dr Mišić a relative of mine was in the infectious diseases ward and I should like to visit him. I explained he had hepatitis to which I was immune. He said there shouldn't be any problems. He gave me a white uniform, saw me to the ward and returned to his institute.

Marko just couldn't believe his eyes when I entered his room. "How on earth did you get in here?" he exclaimed. "Well, love knows no obstacles," I replied, smiling. We hugged and kissed passionately. We had to hurry up because someone could appear at any moment — the captain who shared the room, a nurse or doctor. Still on my feet, I opened my fly and he began sucking my dick, not moving from his bed. He did it with great pleasure, it was obvious that he hadn't done it for a long time and really missed it. I shot my load into his mouth. After washing and tidying up we sat down and talked.

Less than five minutes later Marko's roommate, the young captain, returned to the room. Marko introduced me as one of his relatives and the three of us talked — mostly about hepatitis. What would have happened if he'd returned ten minutes earlier? He'd have caught his roommate giving head to a uniformed doctor (of course, he had no idea who I really was). Having said my goodbyes to Marko and the young captain, I went back to Dr Mišić to return his white coat. As he was not in his office I hung it on a clothes hook. At the gate, I gave in my pass to the guard, took my identity papers and went home.

★★★

The sex I had at the Army Hospital wasn't very exciting in itself but it was exciting for me because of the fact that it took place there. That hospital was for me a symbol of communist elite privilege and of the army which guarded its power. I especially hated the army, the hierarchy, the stiff conservative morality, the anti-homosexual attitude, the old generals and colonels who'd had the privilege of being treated there — including Marshal Tito himself. The hospital was an elite institution of the system and one of the temples of the communist gods. The fact that I was able to sneak into their well-guarded bastion was for me my victory and their defeat. Like a spy or terrorist I had managed to break into their fortress. I felt like Robin Hood who unnoticed got into the castle of the evil Sheriff of Nottingham to save Maid Marion. The high point of my revenge was successfully performing an unnatural act with another man in the dangerous and fortified castle, which is punishable with up to a year in prison under article 110 of the Serbian criminal code.

The thought that Marko and I were probably the only people who'd had homosexual sex in the Army Hospital amused me. In that way we desecrated it. I enjoyed the sex but more than that I enjoyed the secret and symbolic revenge on the system I hated. I will remember this incident till the end of my life. The saying that forbidden fruit is the sweetest is certainly true.

July 6th, 1986

A Product of the Imperialist West

The latest issue of *Reporter* contains an article entitled 'Homosexuality under Socialism', covering the conference on the position of gay people in our society organised by the Centre for Ideological Training of the Youth Organisation. The conference was held despite loud protests from certain high officials of the Organisation. Thus the president of the City Committee said that homosexuality was a product of the Western imperialists who were attempting to infiltrate it into our system of socialist self-management leading to communism. He also said that the conference was nothing but a provocation for healthy socialist personalities because it was being held at the same time as the congress of the Communist Party. He warned: "All responsible persons from the Centre for Ideological Training will be dismissed!"

Among the speakers at the conference were: Jovan Sekulić, a psychologist (who has consistently fought for gay rights); Moma, the non-gay chairperson; Lela, introduced as a 'sexually liberal person' (i.e. a lesbian); and Vita, a 'sexually liberal' gay man. I got so angry with certain things that were said that I put my name down to speak, introducing myself as a 'Belgrade University professor' — not giving my name. Therefore in the *Reporter* article I was referred to as 'a professor'.

Why did I want to speak? Because this Vita, who had recently come to Belgrade from a Bosnian village, and who I already knew, was introduced as a typical representative of gay men. He was a complete ignoramus, an uneducated person who could not speak properly and was also quite effeminate. His looks, gestures, way of speaking and what he said, were just suited to confirm the worst prejudices of the heterosexual public. He seemed to me like a clown, easily exposed to ridicule and jeers. He was an ideal example to prove the intellectual and human inferiority of gay people. What irritated me still more was the nonsense he talked. Among other things, he said: "Jovan [the psychologist] talks about gay organising. Why should we organise ourselves when heterosexuals haven't? Personally, I've not felt any repression in this society. I've never wanted to join an organisation, and I know there are enough men around I can make contact with. When I first came to Belgrade, I felt the environment was quite favourable for us, so I don't hide the fact that I'm homosexual, either at work or elsewhere. In my personal view, I wish men treated girls as well as they treat me."

His statement made me so furious that I said the following (as quoted in the newspaper):

"I find it rather interesting that the organisers have picked a homosexual from a rural environment. I don't want to offend anyone here, but this disgraceful effeminate guy can only help create a very unfavorable image of gay people in the heterosexual public, who already have various prejudices about homosexuality. I am a homosexual and I'm not ashamed to admit it, but I'm also a professor in Belgrade. I'm not saying this to boast, but to prove that no one could tell us apart from straight people. I estimate that ninety per cent of all gays look normal, and I have a lot of experience in this field. I strongly disagree with Vita's theory that we don't need organisation and that all's well the way it is now. Unfortunately things for gay people are very bad and difficult in all respects. Anyway, it takes guts to speak in public although I certainly do not feel as embarrassed as Vita does."

Insulted, Vita replied:

"The gentleman says he resents the fact that it wasn't an intellectual who was invited to speak but somebody, as he put it, from a rural environment. I know he never considered me intelligent, but that didn't prevent him from sleeping with me a couple of years ago... while I was still a minor" (the audience laughed).

When I reflect on the event now it all seems pretty funny. I resent having reacted like that, impulsively and without a second thought. In my efforts to confront straight prejudice I allowed all my scorn and hatred towards effeminate gays to come pouring out. With that I proved I was no better or more tolerant than the wider society. I myself am a victim of the blind hatred for those most different from me whereas I am supposed to fight for mutual tolerance and coexistence.

However my feelings are so strong that despite myself I cannot get rid of my dislike for effeminate homosexuals. When I see them I feel ashamed of being gay. I hate them too because they are usually presented to straight society as typical gays — because of their conspicuousness and intrusiveness. I am ashamed because I feel that straights will think I am like them. Needless to say they also repel me sexually — I am attracted to men not to male parodies of women.

I do not regard effeminate gays as 'true and normal homosexuals', and I often feel the need to challenge their right to represent us gay men. Let them say instead, 'We are effeminate gays and speak only for ourselves, not in the name of all homosexuals'. It would be absurd to take prostitutes as representative of the entire female sex, allowing them to speak for all women. Similarly with gays. One minority subgroup should not be made representative of the whole category.

What irritated me most when I read my statement, though, was the fact that I was so immodest as to present myself as an example of a 'model homosexual'. As opposed to the effeminate peasant who was brought to the conference, here I am, an urbanite, so manly that no one is supposed to notice my homosexuality, and finally, an intellectual — a university professor! That was really tasteless and pretentious. I could have simply sated that there were manly homosexuals, intellectuals and professors — that would have been enough. But no, I had to go out there and show myself off as 'an exquisite specimen of this unknown race'. I was a clown myself, and fun was had by all.

I had another reason for regret when I saw two of my students in the room, who were high-ups in the Youth Organisation and Student Association. So I gave myself away in public, and they learned I was gay. I was afraid all my colleagues would find out, and who knows what consequences it might have on my career.

July 22nd, 1987

A Lost Club

It was a hot night in July. I parked my car, as usual, on Tirš Street, just across from the maternity ward where I happened to be born. I did not get out of the car immediately, I sat inside a little longer to listen to Jennifer Rush's "Power of Love". When the song was finished, I turned off the radio, got out of the car and walked slowly towards the park. I was in a dilemma whether to turn right and take the darker and more dangerous path, or turn left and take the other path, which was partly lit by the streetlights on Yugoslav National Army Boulevard. I decided on the latter. I soon met a group of gays and we said hello to each other. They warned me not to go any further, because there was a policeman waiting in the dark asking everyone who came that way for his identity papers.

I wasn't particularly afraid of meeting the cop, but I try to avoid encounters with the police as a matter of course, so I started walking back to my car. But then I felt like doing something out of spite — after all, I wasn't doing anything illegal by taking a walk in the park at night. I wanted that cop to ask me for my identity papers, I wanted to tell him that I had a perfect right to walk wherever and whenever I wanted and even tell him I was a homosexual if necessary. So I started walking down the dark footpath, towards the place he was supposedly hanging out. There was nobody on the path, everybody had fled. When I passed by the entrance to the Oncology Clinic, I saw him hidden in the dark, wearing a police cap. This was unusual, because they generally remove their caps in the park so as to be less conspicuous. I knew he was looking forward to a victim being caught in his trap.

"Come here," he said in a sharp commanding voice. I approached him and saw he was about twenty-five, a little shorter than me, sturdy, with a rough thick face and dark curly hair. He seemed cold and conceited.

"What are you doing here?"

"Just taking a walk."

"Where're you from?"

"Novi Beograd."

"What are you doing here then?"

"I've just said. I'm taking a walk to freshen myself up, it's too hot inside."

I expected he would ask for my ID, but the conversation took an unexpected direction.

"Do you have a lighter, or some matches?"

"No, I don't. I don't smoke."

"Are you gay?" He finally gathered enough courage to ask me the main question — the one I'd been impatiently waiting for.

"Yeah, I am," I replied calmly.

He was surprised when he heard my answer, probably because most guys he confronted in the park did not own up to the question. He seemed a little confused because things weren't going the way he was used to. This was a new situation for him and he wasn't prepared for it. He was no longer in the position to play the role of a merciless investigator torturing his victim in order to make him admit to being homosexual. I thought he would ask for my ID after my reply, but he went on asking questions.

"So, you like men."

"Yes."

"Do you come here every day?"

"No, just occasionally — two or three times a week."

"You come here to look for men?"

"Yes."

"Are you active in sex, or passive?" Until then, no cop had ever asked me this question.

"Active."

"What do you do with them? Fuck them?"

"Not always. It depends..."

"Do you always take them to your place?"

"Not always. I'm very careful who I take back to my apartment."

"You have an apartment ?"

"Yes, I do."

"Do you live alone?"

"Yes."

"How did you get the apartment?"

"I didn't 'get' it, I bought it."

"Well, well! You're lucky if you earn that sort of money."

"Well, I do work hard."

"What's your job then?"

"I'm a university professor."

"You — a professor!" He stared at me in disbelief.

"How old are you?"

"Thirty-seven." He looked me in the face, to check if I was telling the truth.

"Well, you look younger. So, you're a university professor!"

What he meant was that it was quite impossible for a faggot to be a university professor.

"Yes."

"How much is your salary?"

"Not much. About 23 million dinars."

"Well, well! It's not that small!"

"How much is yours? I've heard that policemen are quite well-paid nowadays."

"No way. It's miserable." He did not want to say how much his salary was. Then I started my 'counter-offensive' by asking him questions. He hesitated to answer because he obviously wasn't used to being on the other side in an interrogation.

"Where are you from?" I asked, as if interested.

"From Doboj." So, he was from Bosnia, just like I thought.

"How long have you been here in Belgrade?"

"Six years."

"Where do you live? At the singles hostel?"

"Yes."

"Do you pay for your accommodation there? It's probably very cheap."

"Yes."

"Do you get free food?"

"No. Only one meal when we're on duty."

"What is your daily working time?"

"I work eight hours every day."

"How old are you?"

"Twenty-four."

"Are you going to stay in Belgrade, or will they transfer you?"

"It depends. I'll stay if I get married."

While we were talking, an unshaven, sweaty man wearing wrinkled pyjamas approached us. I was obvious that he was a patient from one of the nearby hospitals. He was shouting, "Ivan! Ivan!"

"What are you doing here, comrade?" the policeman asked him.

"We're looking for a patient. He ran away from the hospital and he was supposed to have an operation tomorrow."

"Who allowed you to do so?" asked my policeman, as if you needed a special permit to look for someone in the park.

"Well, a nurse did. Another patient and I are looking for him."

"What hospital did he run from?" I joined in the conversation.

"This one here." He pointed at the grey, depressing building.

"From the Oncology Clinic?"

"Yeah."

"Okay, pal, you can go," the cop said, interrupting the conversation. He turned back to me. "A lot of things are going on here," he continued.

"Yes, quite a lot." I put a particular stress on 'a lot', pointing at the ambiguity of the sentence, but I don't think he understood.

"Have you ever had sex with a woman?" he resumed the conversation.

"Oh yes, several times." I lied to make everything more acceptable to him; I'd had sex with a woman only once.

"Do you ever intend to get married?"

"I don't know. Not yet anyway. Maybe later." I lied once again, as I had no intention at all to marry.

"Don't you feel less masculine when you have sex with men?"

"No, quite the contrary. I feel twice a man when I have sex with men. If a man is stronger and, of course, much manlier than a woman, fucking him is automatically a sign of greater masculinity than fucking a weak woman. Don't you think so?"

"But it's unnatural."

"It isn't. It's as natural as having sex with a woman. The most famous sexologists and scientists such as Hirschfeld, Weininger, Freud, Marcuse, Kinsey and others think that humans are essentially bisexual. That means that there's a potential in each of us to be both heterosexual and homosexual. Judeo-Christian morality is to be blamed for the fact that homosexuality has been 'pushed out' from human nature and put under a ban." He had a vacuous expression, as he was unfamiliar with Freud, Marcuse, Judeo-Christian morality and other things I mentioned — I knew things were going well for me. He made no comment, and had no counter-arguments.

A fat man with a beard came out of the dark, wearing white shorts and a striped shirt. I immediately recognised Popadija.

"Do you have a match?" the cop asked him.

"Yes."

"Give it to me, I want to light up this bush. I've lost something."

"Here, take the whole box," Popadija said, handing him the box with an ironic smile on his face. The cop took the box of matches and lit one after another, trying to find something in the bushes.

"What have you lost?" I asked, curious.

"I threw something at a guy who managed to run away."

"Oh."

"Here, thanks. There's one match left. You can go," he said to Popadija and let him go without asking him for his identity papers. I still did not know what the thing he lost was, so I asked him again: "Well, what exactly have you lost?"

"My baton! I tried to hit him with it and it fell somewhere

here in the bushes. Let's try to find it together. You look here, and I'll look over there." The situation was so hilarious that I almost burst out laughing. The cop had lost his baton, the symbol of his power. I looked for it where I was told and soon found it. It was right under the light from the street lamp, not in the bushes at all. I couldn't believe he wasn't able to find it by himself.

"Here, I've found it!" I said, handing him the baton. He didn't look at all surprised but just took it silently from me and hung it on his belt. We talked some more but I decided to leave as I wanted to find someone for sex.

"Well, I really have to go," I said, offering him my hand.

"Wait. Can you give me a lift back to my precinct? I have to be there by eleven." I'd already told him I had a car.

"Okay." I agreed because it is not sensible to refuse one of our police officers, especially if they ask a favour so politely. Nevertheless the situation was a bit confused and suspicious. I suspected he had some hidden intentions.

When we got in my car and started our way down Tirš Street towards Sarajevska Street, he suddenly started squeezing my right thigh, and said in an excited, rasping voice, as if he was afraid that someone might hear, "I'd like to do it with a man! I never have! When we get to the precinct, I'm free. Let's go to your place."

Although I hoped that something like that would happen, I didn't expect his suppressed, 'illegal' impulses to be revealed so soon. However, I was afraid things were going too smoothly, suspecting that he only wanted to provoke me, and that if I agreed to have sex with him he would accuse me of seducing an officer and take me into custody. Therefore I was extremely careful, trying to decline his offer for the time being, but not to discourage and offend him. So, I started my game.

"I don't know what to say. You're a policeman, after all. I've never done it with a cop."

"So you feel uncomfortable because of that."

"Yes, I don't know if you really want it. Are you positive about it? I wouldn't like to make you resent anything later."

"But I do want to do it — I'm sure about it!"

"I really don't know what to say. Perhaps it's better for

you not to get involved in these things. You are a policeman. You should be very careful about what you do."

By then we were already quite near the precinct, and it was time for me to say goodbye to him for tonight. He told me to park my car some hundred metres from the precinct.

"I'm going to change my clothes. Wait for me here!"

"Sorry, but I really can't tonight. My brother's coming over for the night. Look — here's my phone number, give me a call tomorrow or the day after. We can make a date then." He was surprised and obviously disappointed that I'd refused him. It had taken a lot of effort and courage on his part to actually ask a gay man for sex. And the guy had refused him! He most probably expected every homosexual to accept his offer. He took down my phone number nervously.

"Okay. I don't know if I'll be in a position to call you. I'll think about it. Bye," he said haughtily. It was pretty obvious he was angry and shaken by the way things had turned out.

"Bye," I said, with a smile which revealed self-satisfaction.

★★★

July 25th, 1987

The cop I met in the park called me today. We made a date to meet in front of Hotel Slavija at six o'clock. When I arrived there he was already waiting for me. I was completely disappointed. He wasn't wearing his uniform, just his ordinary clothes. In my eyes more than half of his sex appeal was gone. He seemed clean and well-shaven and wore a light blue Lacoste shirt (probably a 'made in Turkey' one sold at low prices by smugglers), bad quality jeans without a label and a pair of black, old-fashioned pointed-toe shoes deformed by his big feet. He was also wearing white socks. Dressed like that he simply didn't attract me at all. Nevertheless, as he was there, and as I had wanted to make it with a cop for a long time (even though my fantasies related only to the uniform) I decided to take him back to my place.

We had a stupid and forced conversation. He was quite

silent and nervous. Arriving at my flat, I gave him a brandy and put on a heterosexual porn video to make him relax. We watched it in total silence. I waited for him to take the initiative. I didn't move a finger and wanted to torture him for a while. It wasn't long before he started touching me. He pinched me, squeezed me, bit me and hugged me, groaning and panting with excitement. He was also sweating a lot, something I found quite repulsive.

When we undressed and moved to the bed he continued biting and squeezing me. It was quite unpleasant and painful and his big bovine body was disgustingly sweaty. As soon as we finished having sex we dressed and I gave him a lift to the city.

August 29th, 1987

Under Buddha's Protection

I took a walk in Kalemegdan, hoping to meet somebody for sex, like I usually do on Sunday afternoons. I was most interested in soldiers and boys from provincial towns, who seem to wander about with no actual destination, and gladly accept the conversation and company of a stranger. I usually put my watch in my pocket and ask them the time. I then decide whether there's any point pursuing the conversation or not, from the way they answer my questions (sharp, crude, hostile, friendly etc.). If I conclude that there is a fair chance of having them, I ask them where they come from, how long they've been in the army and in Belgrade, what their jobs are, and so on. Then, if things go well, I invite them back to my place for a drink, saying casually that I have some good porno videos. A few, who are suspicious, refuse my offer; others accept, knowing in advance what's in store. Then there's a third group — the naive ones — who accept my invitation without suspecting anything.

This Sunday, I saw a soldier standing alone on the ridge near the Observatory, looking over at the landscape in Novi Beograd and Ušce. I stood beside him, not too near, however, and started similarly gazing at the scenery. Then I casually started a conversation.

"Excuse me, do you have the time?" I asked him, acting as if I was in a hurry.

"Ten past three," he said, reading the numbers on his cheap digital watch.

"Where do you come from?"

"Vitez, in Bosnia."

"How long have you been in the army?"

"Three months."

"In Belgrade?"

"A month now."

"What's your job when you're not in the army?"

"I'm a car mechanic."

"Where are you going now?"

"Just out walking. Seeing the sights. I see something new every time I go out. It'll be cold in the winter, so I won't be able to get out so much."

"Are you free at the moment?"

"Yeah, I am."

"If you want, we could go to my place for a drink. I've also got some good porno videos. How about it?"

"Yeah, let's go," he said without any hesitation or additional questions. I had the distinct impression he had no idea what I wanted from him.

When we got back to my place, I deliberately asked him to take his shoes off, because my carpet is light pink and gets dirty easily — though in fact, I hate the habit of removing your shoes when entering an apartment. It was part of my scenario for him. I knew that he probably had smelly feet (in summer feet usually sweat a lot in army boots), and this would give me a reason to ask him to wash his feet or even take a shower. That's just what happened; his feet were smelly and after a short conversation I asked him to take a shower. He didn't want to at first but I insisted and he finally agreed.

I told him to take off his uniform in the living room so that it wouldn't get wet in the bathroom. I hoped he would remove the rest of his clothes too. However, he only removed his shirt and trousers and kept on his boxer shorts (these I find unattractive as I prefer slip briefs, boxer shorts always strike me as bit unsanitary). He then went into the bathroom. Through the ventilation hole on the lower part of the bathroom door I could see what he was doing. He undressed and I could see that he had a good body. He sat on the toilet with his legs spread wide, facing towards the wall, and pissed. When I tried to get in I found that he'd locked the door. This meant he was either bashful or in fact had a premonition about what I wanted.

I pushed the door some more and after a few moments he opened it but he'd put on his shorts. I told him I only wanted to wash my hands; he could get on with his shower and close the shower curtains over the bath. While I was taking rather a long time to wash my hands he got into the bath dressed in his shorts, pulled the curtain, but not all the way, and then removed the offending shorts. As he couldn't adjust the tap to get warm water I used that as an excuse to pull the curtain back to help him. When he started showering I undressed and got in the shower with him saying how smelly I was and how I could do with a shower too. He made no comment. I did all the talking, at the same time rubbing him with soap, first his neck and down to his chest and belly, then all the way to his arse, cock and thighs. He didn't resist so I asked him to reciprocate. He did it nicely and started rubbing my thighs and cock at his own initiative which encouraged me to start kissing him. I pushed my tongue into his mouth and he did the same to me. We rubbed each other with the soap and hugged and kissed for a while. After a bit he said we'd better go back into the living room.

We went into the room wearing bathrobes, and lay on the bed watching pornos. Of course I played a straight video. While we were watching we continued to hug and kiss, pushing our tongues deep into each other's mouths. This lasted for about ten minutes and then he asked me to stop the video and put on some slow music. That sounded to me like a signal that he wanted more serious sex. I told him to choose a cassette from the bookcase by the window. As he didn't find anything suitable I went over to search together with him. I asked him if he had chosen something.

"Yes, I have," he said sharply. His voice sounded somehow strange and hoarse with a note of irony in it. The expression on his face had also changed. I felt that something was wrong, but what happened next was beyond my expectations. I moved towards the bed instinctively, turning my back on him for just a moment, and felt a blow to my head. I turned around and saw him looking furious and holding my metal vase from India, with which he had just hit me.

"What do you think, that I'm a faggot?" he shouted angrily.

"Do you want a fight?" I shouted back, trying to look as brave as I could, and not show how afraid I really was. With my right hand I seized a heavy bronze statuette of Buddha from the bookshelf. It became my weapon against the metal vase in his hand. At that moment I felt something warm running down my body. I looked at myself and found I was covered in blood flowing from the wound on my head. I was stricken with panic. I realised I was an easy prey, being naked and wounded, and decided it was better if I didn't try and fight with him. After all it was me who was losing blood, not him. He could injure me easily with the sharp edge of the vase he was holding, if I didn't faint any moment from the loss of blood.

So I made a quick escape towards the window. I jumped over the railing and stepped out on the plinth which goes around our floor. I went to my next-door neighbours' balcony and called out to them to open their door for me. When they opened it and saw me naked and covered in blood they were flabbergasted. They gave me some old pyjamas to put on. They didn't ask me anything, partly because they were so shocked and partly because they suspected that something obscure and obscene had happened. I told them to call the police.

While they were dialling the number I went back the same way to my balcony to see what was going on in my apartment. As I could see nobody in my room I supposed that he was either in the bathroom getting dressed or had already left. I stepped inside carefully. Fortunately for me the car mechanic had fled. I went back to my neighbours quickly to tell them not to call the police. They were already talking to someone and I asked them to hang up. Having the cops round was all I needed to complete a perfect day.

Quickly I put on my clothes, got into my car and rushed to the hospital. I was afraid I might have internal bleeding or even a cerebral haemorrhage. They received me at the casualty clinic without any haste. They took my health insurance papers and told me to sit in the waiting-room. After a while, they called me in. A nurse washed my wound and shaved a part of my head around it. Then a young blond doctor sewed the wound in the way you mend an old torn sock. Finally they X-rayed my head. They told me that my skull wasn't broken and there was no internal bleeding because I hadn't lost consciousness and I wasn't sleepy.

I was quite lucky because he could have killed me. If he'd picked up the heavy bronze Buddha instead of the light metal vase he would have smashed my skull. And if I had fainted he would have been able to finish me off in his fury. I had been quite near to death, but this time too I had stayed alive. Probably as foolish as ever but, nevertheless, alive. The fact that he'd taken the vase and not the Buddha made think it was all God's will. As if God wanted the soldier to hit me but not to kill me. It was a message from Him, and I understood it as a kind of warning which told me I should be more careful, give up promiscuity and turn to more serious things.

I wasn't mad at the guy who tried to kill me. He was just an instrument in the hands of a higher force — destiny. On the other hand, however, he too was a victim of a homophobic society which had implanted a great fear of homosexuality and hatred towards it in his super-ego.

This phenomenon is described and labelled in psychology as homosexual panic. In such cases, sexual intercourse is often started or even finished normally, but then the seduced heterosexual gets a seizure of this panic. During such seizures, he is capable of killing the homosexual who seduced him. Such murders are committed while the murderer is temporarily insane, as his mind is blinded with hatred. Killers of this kind do not usually intend to kill before they actually do so. They are usually normal, sane individuals, but with such a hatred toward their own and others' homosexuality implanted in their minds by society, that they react furiously in this way. The soldier from Bosnia was a typical example of this kind of panic. In a normal situation he was probably a good boy. He didn't take anything from my apartment, although he had the opportunity to steal a lot of things after I had escaped through the window. But he was in the position to become an 'innocent' murderer for nothing, instead of having relaxed and enjoyable sex. The social norms in his head prevented him from doing so and nearly resulted in murder.

October 14th, 1987

Bloody Nose Ejaculation

We visited Dad at the hospital again. They told him he should have a third rectoscopy. This time they will have to use a thinner and more flexible probe tube which can get deeper into his colon. They need to see the size of the polyp and if there are any more. I have the impression that he's given himself up to his fate and to the hospital machinery. He comes out of hospital on Friday to spend the weekend at home and returns on Monday.

I came back home around five in the afternoon. I went to bed to take a nap and read the newspapers, waiting for a cadet from the military academy to call. I met him the other day in front of the Yugoplastika shop on Prince Mihajlo Street. He asked me the time and I used it as a cue to start a conversation. He said he was from Macedonia, although he did not have the Macedonian accent at all. He had short dark hair, a plump and firm body and the look of a sportsman, but his attitude was cold. His face was not especially beautiful — he had a big crooked nose. I liked him however and he made an erotic impact on me. I expected him to stop the conversation soon and leave.

Nevertheless the conversation went on, with some interruptions and breaks, and he still stood beside me. It seemed a bit suspicious to me, so I decided to quicken things by cutting the futile talk. I asked him where he was going and he replied that he was off to the cinema to see *Jaws* in 3-D. "What a shame — I intended to invite you to my place to look at some porno videos," I told him. His eyes opened wide. I gave him my number to call me up. He called today and we made a date to meet in front of the Albanija building at seven o'clock.

★★★

We met at the appointed time. He was wearing a leather jacket, check trousers and patent leather shoes. We went to my car. On the way he told me he couldn't leave the barracks earlier because they were being visited by General Mamula, the defence minister. The lad said he belonged to an elite unit so he had to stay longer because of an inspection.

When we got to my flat, even before I opened the door, he stooped down to take off his shiny shoes. He entered the flat without his shoes — how I hate that custom! — so I gave him a pair of slippers. I offered him a glass of brandy and some bananas. We sat and talked. I kept the conversation going, asking him questions, although I was not really interested in most of the answers, only those which ignited his interest and pleasure allowing the conversation to flow and develop. They were all about the army and his own activities in it.

He told me he was from a small village in Macedonia and that he enrolled in the military academy in Belgrade when he was only fifteen — this explained his accent-free Serbian. He was a good swimmer, he said he swam I don't know how many seconds or tenths of seconds faster than the republic or federal record, I again don't know which. He was a tank driver although he wasn't particularly satisfied with it at first. He told me enthusiastically that the motor of a domestic tank has a piston displacement of 12,000 cubic centimetres, that we supposedly managed to cheat on the Russians and get a licence for the tank T-72, instead of the T-65. After certain preparations, those tanks can go under water, along the bottom of a river for example. He told me that a column of tanks is protected on its head and sides by special vehicles with anti-tank weapons, that anti-tank guns have a range of up to six kilometres and other anti-tank weapons only two to five hundred metres, that there is very little room inside a tank, etc. When I'd run out of questions and after I had answered the few questions he put to me, who I live with, what I do and so on, I decided to get to the point.

I suggested that we watch porno videos. He accepted the

suggestion with pleasure, seemingly not anticipating anything. I waited for a certain period, then I placed my hand on his thigh. He did not react. Then I put my hand on his fly and grasped it. The gesture was accompanied by my words in a forcibly humorous tone, "It's not stiff yet, you're not reacting?" "No!" he replied somehow absentmindedly. I felt I should not go any further. He was fascinated by the porno images shimmering on the screen, but he did not respond in a sexual way, his cock was not hard at all. Probably in order to keep my hands off him he moved a bit away from me and put an ashtray on his thigh. It remained there even when he extinguished his cigarette. Suddenly he started sniffling as if he'd caught a cold. I didn't say anything about it so as not to interrupt his attention. When I got fed up with this tense and rather hopeless situation, I switched off the video and turned on the lights. Then I saw he was not sniffling because of a cold but because of a nose bleed. Instead of a hard-on and a discharge through spraying sperm, blood ran out of his nose. It was a bloody nasal orgasm.

★★★

Later I explained this strange phenomenon to myself in theoretical terms, with help from Klaus Theweleit's book *Male Fantasies*. Among other things he writes about relations between the (homo)sexuality of soldiers and military drill. According to his theory, which did not seem very plausible at first, soldiers exert themselves during hard training and rigid drills in such a way that at certain moments of either strain or relaxation there is a loss of consciousness and/or a bleeding nose, while the body is in a state similar to orgasm. Instead of releasing the libidinous energy through ejaculation and relaxation they lose consciousness (I was lucky he didn't pass out in my flat), or their noses bleed, while the whole body functions as a phallus which ejaculates. So, that is what happened to my cadet. His body was a phallus ejaculating blood through his nose. As I realised from our earlier conversation that he had problems approaching girls, it was clear he was in a sexual sense constantly tense and frustrated.

January 29th, 1988

A Lucky Cook

I met Dejan, a guy from Obrenovac, at the railway station toilet. He had a band-aid on his head, above his temple. His face was all blue and scratched. I asked him, "What happened? Who did this to you?"

He laughed and answered, "Don't ask! I had a fight with some friends of mine. One of them hit me with a bottle of beer on the head."

"You were lucky, if he'd hit you on the temple, you would've been killed!" We talked some more, standing in front of the sinks, then he whispered to me, "Do you want a blow-job?" I said yes, because he turned me on. He looked like a macho hoodlum, and besides he gave passionate blow-jobs. It seems that he also found me attractive and that he didn't do it just for money. I gave him a sign with my head to go into a booth, but he wouldn't do it there, because he was probably afraid someone would peep through a hole in the door. He suggested we went to Milija's. When we got there, we found Saša, an old friend of Milija's who looked more like a woman than a man. We talked, drank coffee and watched TV. Dejan repeated the story of how he was hit with a beer bottle on the head.

Then we started talking about the nicest way to die. We all agreed that the best way was the 'royal death', death during sex. Milija said he knew of two such cases. One of them happened to an acquaintance of his, a cook, who was very fat, and who died while being fucked by a guy. When he saw him dead the guy got really scared and ran away. The main protagonist in the other case was also a fat cook. One evening he was fucked by a guy with a huge prick. After the guy was gone, the fat cook went to sleep and never woke up again. In the morning they found him lying in a pool of blood. The guy who'd fucked him had torn his intestines with his enormous cock so that he'd bled to death during the night. Milija said it was the kind of death he'd gladly choose for himself. It really was a bit of a morbid story and I think a humiliating death, but nevertheless a nice one. From sex you go to sleep, from sleep to death. Wasn't the cook a lucky man!

Since Saša didn't seem like he was about to leave soon, Dejan and I went to the bathroom because he was in a hurry. He gave me a long, juicy blow-job. I wanked off while he was licking my balls. I gave him ten deutschmark. He went off immediately. I stayed there a bit longer then went into the centre to get something to eat.

★★★

I went to the bus station again. I met Neša the Chetnik (I call him that because he supports the extreme rightist parties led by 'Duke' Šešelj and that butcher, Jovič) in front of the toilets. We smuggled ourselves into the toilets, without paying the cleaning ladies. Neša stood next to an interesting young man. I thought they would leave together, since they were both young, and leave me empty-handed. However, after some time, Neša approached me and said the guy wouldn't go with him. Then I decided to try my luck. The guy was on his way out and I followed him. He went towards the railway station toilets, but he couldn't go in as they were closed for repairs. He leant against a pillar on the platform and lit up a cigarette. He had a beard, which I didn't like, but I was attracted by his strong, sturdy body. His face was somehow strange, a bit rough, but he didn't seem like a hooligan. He wore a jacket and tight jeans which neatly contoured his firm arse. We kept looking at each other for a while, then I approached him and asked him where he was from. He answered all my questions. First he said that before moving to Belgrade, he had lived in Ljubljana and Titograd. His father was a mathematician, and he studied at law school. Besides that he also danced at the Abrašević folklore dance club.

I couldn't help laughing quietly when he said that. I knew many guys who danced for these dance clubs. They seem to be 'centres of perversion'. The guy seemed quite intelligent and clever. He accepted my invitation immediately, without a second thought or hesitation.

When we got to my place, he took off his shoes and jacket. I smelled a slight smell of his sweat. I gave him some vodka. Later I made tea for both of us. First we talked about various things, then he went to the bathroom. While he was having a shower, I undressed and went to bed. He came out of the bathroom with a towel wrapped around his hips. He lay beside me. We caressed very gently. We were both enjoying it intensely as if our bodies were in communication by themselves without any deliberate help. He was prepared to have anal sex, but I avoided it from fear of AIDS. I didn't feel like spoiling such gentle sex by trying to put on a condom and all the unpleasant things which go along with it. I wanted him to give me a blow-job but he declined.

I discovered that 'safe sex' can also be exciting and interesting, and concluded that I had to change my behaviour concerning sex. After we'd wanked off, we lay embraced for a long time. He lit a cigarette. It was just like in a film. After making love, happy lovers are lying embraced, and talking. We didn't talk much. I didn't know what to talk about any more. I was bored and getting nervous. I began to look forward to him leaving. I went to the bathroom, took a shower and dressed, in order to show him that he should do the same and go. He received my message. He dressed and went away. Before he left, I gave him my phone number.

October 6th, 1988

My Best Friend

I dreamt of Vlada last night. In my dream, he phoned to tell me to come on over to his place, which was not the house where he used to live, but another one with marble staircases and iron banisters. He waited for me in front of the front door, with a smile on his face. He was young and beautiful in the dream, wearing his famous hairstyle which made him look like a bristling cat, just like a long time ago, when we went to school together, not as fat as he is nowadays. We greeted each other, talked for a while, and then he started showing me his new apartment. He took me to his bedroom which contained a large bed. He took his clothes off, sat on the bed, spread his legs and told me to suck his cock. When I began to do it, the dream was over — it's always like that in dreams, they finish at the very moment when the most beautiful things are about to happen.

I met Vlada when we were in the sixth grade of primary school. That's when I moved with my parents to Cvijićeva Street from another part of town. I also had to go to another school. Vlada and I made friends quite soon, and we shortly became what people call best friends, not only because we attended the same classes and lived pretty near to each other, but also because we had many common interests, plans, and shared the same teenage dreams. My first memories of him reach all the way back to the time when he had short, bristly blond hair and freckles on his face. He used to wear yellowy-brown velvet shorts without a fly, T-shirts and sandals (that's how I remember him most of the time). I liked him more than any other guy in my class. He was one of the cleverest and most restless children in the class. I was attracted to him physically as early as that but I was not particularly aware of it. He was taller, stronger, cleverer and more handsome than me. He got A's, I got B's. Everybody liked him and adored him in a way, schoolkids as well as teachers, whereas I was an average lad who lived in his shadow. His father died when he was just a baby. He lived with his mother, a French teacher, and his sister, on Stanoja Glavaša Street, but his windows faced Cvijicéva Street.

I cannot remember the exact moment when we met or how we became close friends, but I can still recall some of the episodes of our life together. We both hated our country, the communist system, the mentality here, school, etc., and we both planned to flee to America one day and get rich there. We wanted to become famous formula-one racing drivers. He infected me with his love of cars. We used to buy all the Yugoslav car magazines and, when we could, the rare foreign ones too. We used to read them for hours with awe, like we were leafing through the Holy Book, and fantasised about sports cars we were unable to see around us. Later we started frequenting car races, first the ones held around Kalemegdan, then those held in Ušće. We dreamt of visiting Monza or Le Mans one day.

As we wanted to go joyriding so badly we decided to steal a small Fiat 600. We went out armed with screwdrivers, pliers and wires, although we really had no idea of how to use these tools. We'd heard how you could steal a car, but neither of us had any first-hand experience. We picked a car, but whenever a passer-by came along, we'd run away. The idea of stealing a car on New Year's Eve was very silly because the streets were more crowded than usual. Of course our plan failed and we didn't manage to steal any car.

Once, we decided to flee to Italy. We persuaded our parents to let us go to the seaside by ourselves. We said that we were going to Istria and would take a couple of day trips to Trieste. This was our 'official version' but in fact we intended to emigrate and stay in Italy. We wanted to buy a cheap car there — we knew what the prices were from an Italian car magazine — and to roam the Italian autostradas. The fact that we were minors and had no driving licence didn't bother us much. We didn't realise any of our grand plans. We hung around

Trieste for a couple of days, bought some clothes — T-shirts, jeans — mostly in the Ponte Rosso open-air market and the shops nearby, and having spent all our money returned home to Yugoslavia.

We were inseparable in Belgrade, we saw each other every day. Our class teacher even called our parents to tell them that we spent too much time together, neglecting the rest of the class, and to advise them to forbid us to see each other so often. Despite this we remained inseparable, going out together to the cinema, and on day trips to Topčider, Avala, etc. I liked going to the airport most of all because aeroplanes were the second-best things in our hearts. To us they seemed miracles of high technology connecting us to the unreachable, faraway world we constantly dreamt about. We would watch the planes take off for Paris, London or New York, dreaming of going there ourselves one day.

We often went to the airport to watch the planes. Usually we went along the motorway so as to admire the foreign limousines. Sometimes we hitch-hiked and quite often someone would pick us up. We even got a lift from an English diplomat who was driving a big green Vauxhall. We sat back on the soft leather seats and enjoyed ourselves. We especially liked a dim green light which lit up the dashboard.

The new airport in Surčin seemed to us like a foreign enclave — a window through which you could view the whole world because of all the foreign planes, limousines and foreigners arriving and departing. We used to walk around the airport building observing planes from the terrace. During the summer we often sat on the haystacks placed near the fence along the runways. There we were able to observe planes taking off and landing at close quarters, recognising different types of planes and the liveries of different airline companies. Most of the time we wore only our slips or were stark naked. This added an erotic touch to our adventures though I was unaware of the full implications at the time. We also used to go to Ada island in the summer. We would find hidden places and strip off. To start with we were each a bit ashamed to take our clothes off in the other's presence. But as I got more and more interested in seeing him naked I started posing naked before him whenever I got the opportunity so as to set an example and give him the opportunity to do the same. That worked. From then on we saw each other naked quite often.

I have the most pleasant memories of our first physical contacts and sexual experiences. To start with, we teased each other by tugging at each other's zippers — attempting to feel what was inside with our fingers. We even tore each other's trousers once by doing that. The naive story we made up for our parents was that we'd been attacked by older boys. We also used to wrestle to see who was strongest — though we both knew he was the stronger and he always won. First we would wrestle with our clothes on and later when alone at home we used to strip and wear just our underpants. While wriggling around the floor our naked bodies would touch and our arms and legs would intertwine. I wanted to stay in that position, snuggling up to him, for as long as possible. He noticed this once so he asked me if I wanted to wrestle just to be able to touch him. I cannot remember my answer though I probably denied it. He never asked that question again although our wrestling continued.

We started taking baths together whenever we were alone. We used to light the fire in the old steam boiler with old newspapers — there were no electric heaters at the time — fill the tub with hot water and get in together. I remember the time I took a snorkel and put my head into the water while he sat facing me. I pretended I was a sea-bed explorer. I examined his body closely under the water, paying close attention to his cock. I played with it imagining it to be a fish. Finally, at a more mature stage in our sexual relationship we took up masturbating. Most of the time we would masturbate each other or just help each other by rubbing each other's balls or the perineum. We both liked that very much. I tended to initiate our mutal masturbation more often than not. Once we were laying on the bed and simulated intercourse between a man and a woman just for fun. He knelt over me and placed his cock right in front of my mouth. At the time however I was ignorant of sexual techniques and not at all familiar with oral sex, so nothing happened. That stage of our teenage sexuality was the most beautiful sexual period in my life. Never again have I felt such a joy and excitement with sex.

I remember us shoplifting together. On one such occasion we stole a bottle of Racke whisky from a supermarket on Čika Ljubina Street. While he was attracting the shop assistant's attention I took the bottle and hid it in my jacket. I managed to leave the supermarket without being noticed. When he joined me outside we were overwhelmed with joy — we had triumphed, we had won. To us our shoplifting was not immoral or dishonourable but an act of courage and revenge on the society we both hated. My other motive was to gain his respect for my bravery. Once we wanted this small plastic racing-car model displayed in a kiosk. We made elaborate plans on how to steal it, we loitered near the kiosk thinking what to do. Then I decided to act all by myself. I asked the assistant to let me see the toy. As soon as I took hold of it I ran as quickly as I could. The assistant cried out, "Thief!" and I was even chased by someone for a while, but I managed to escape. As Vlada was the one who initiated and planned our thefts while I was a mere accessory or a perpetrator, this action, thoroughly conceived and performed by me, really made me more respectable in his eyes.

I almost depended on him, I adored him without being aware of it. I felt really bad every time we quarrelled, especially when he was mad at me for days and he did not want to see or phone me. I was also very jealous of all the boys and girls he spoke to. I wanted him to be all mine. During sports lessons when he removed his T-shirt I experienced real seizures of jealousy because others would see his body. I wanted to be the only person privileged enough to see him naked. I was desperate, not wanting to share anything of him with anyone else. I knew many girls in our class were in love with him. He didn't care for girls for a long time, regarding them as a sort of 'lower species'. However, his attitude gradually changed and he became quite interested in them. I grew desperate and regarded his behaviour as a betrayal. Now, he started using his stripping off during physical education as a means of seducing them. Those in love with him started to write him poems and love letters, sending secret messages and so on. Nevertheless he was still inseparable from me and he still despised the girls in our class. I managed to keep him by my side until the third grade of secondary school. Then he fell in love with a girl called Maja, who went to another school and was even older than him. He was proud of being with her whereas to me she seemed like a cheap whore. I found her repulsive the first time I met her — a coquette and nymphomaniac. It was the beginning of the end of our close friendship.

In Freudian terms he had left the so-called homosexual stage of development behind him, while I stayed in it for my whole life. Gradually we got more alienated from each other and stopped seeing each other so often. We enrolled at different universities and I went abroad with my parents, spending four years out of the country. He dated Maja for almost six years. He was completely nuts about her at first as she really charmed him. She had full control of him, wrapping him around her little finger, and he followed her around like a little dog.

Later they switched roles, he gradually became colder to her so she tried desperately to keep him by her side. She cried, begged, tried to slash her wrists, but he eventually left her. He studied film and joined a theatrical company. He became a real Don Juan, but took up drinking and became quite fat. He wears a beard now so there is no trace any more of his boyish good looks and slimness. With his beard he reminds me of Hemingway. We corresponded for a while when I was in Switzerland, and we saw each other on my short trips back to Belgrade. However we were completely alienated from each other and so gradually we lost contact. I heard he'd married a woman from Dubrovnik and had settled there. They had two sons. I never knew if he was sober for long enough to ever graduate from university and then, during that period, the last time I saw him he was fat, bearded and his face was swollen with alcohol.

★★★

October 1993

Since I wrote the above notes, Vlada has returned to Belgrade. He'd been forced to flee from Dubrovnik with his family very quickly. They escaped when the siege and bombardment of the town began. The town was under siege by the former Yugoslav army. The two main nationalities in the town were Serbs and Coats. The treatment of Serbs was unbearable because the Croats vented all their fury on them. Vlada and his family were threatened with death so he was forced to return to Belgrade together with his Croat wife and sons. I came across him on a street and he hardly recognised me. He had lost some weight and his face looked a lot older. He seemed somehow absent-minded and lost — not surprising after what he'd been through. We talked in a formal way for a couple of minutes, exchanging such phrases as "how are you doing?", "how's your family?" and so on. We promised to see each other soon to catch up on our news, but he hasn't called me and neither have I. I heard that he and his family were living in his mother's apartment for a while but now have their own flat. I also saw him in a TV commercial playing the role of an elegant client of a savings bank — the bank went under soon after.

November 14th, 1988

A Bricklayer

The latest issue of *Start* magazine contains a long article about a maniac who raped boys. Here are the most important parts of the article without any comments of my own:

"A bricklayer called Dragan Cvenić, born September 28th, 1956 in Valpevo, will be tried in court. This quiet man who lived alone in an old house in the suburbs of Valpovo was, as they say, a good worker who could lay bricks much faster than his colleagues. We found out that he wasn't married, he finished only four grades of primary education during which he didn't even learn to write and he was also declared unfit for military service, so he didn't go into the army. The investigator of the case points out that 'the accused has been retarded in his mental process since childhood', to which a 'psychotic mental process similar to schizophrenia, apparent in his dissociation of thoughts' is added.

"Dragan Cvenić lured young boys, one at a time, or groups of them, into his house, with the intention of performing unnatural sexual activities with them. He ordered them to strip naked, tied them to a bed or to the door of his room with ropes or chains, and then laid them on the bed and performed sexual activities with them using force. Later, he gave them presents or money, threatening them not to tell anyone... Cvenić admits to doing the same unnatural acts with three more minors aged between eight and sixteen, who as he says accepted his perverse suggestions. Sometimes he was 'on the top', and sometimes 'on the bottom'... It is assumed that there were about two hundred cases of such criminal actions against a person's dignity and against morality. Those boys would keep going back to the bricklayer's, and he would again perform violence on their minds and bodies, but he was eventually caught by the police. The boys didn't turn him in. Therefore no one had stopped these perverse orgies of this man-next-door from a hill above the river."

November 17th, 1988

A Boy With Chocolate

A nice, brown-haired boy of about seventeen stopped in front of the window of the Obuća shoe shop on Prince Mihajlo Street. He wore jeans and a denim jacket with white fake fur. He unwrapped a Nestle's chocolate bar from its red wrapper. I wondered whether I should approach him or not, but decided to wait until he had eaten the chocolate. I didn't want to interrupt him while his mouth was full. I remembered Pessoa's poem 'Street Stand' , which could also be applied to this boy eating his candy with such pleasure. I have to quote at least part of this poem; since I first read it, I always remember these lines when I eat chocolate:

> Eat the chocolate, little girl!
> Eat the chocolate!
> See that there is no metaphysics in this world
>   beside the chocolate.
> See that all religions do not teach more than
>   a candy store.
> Eat, you little dirty thing, eat!
> If only I could eat so truly as you do.
> But I think, and when I take off the silver
>   paper, actually made of tin,
> I throw everything on the ground, like I've thrown
>   away life.

After he'd eaten half the chocolate, he put the rest back in his bag and slowly started towards Kalemegdan. Then I approached him, using my old, well-tested scenario. I told him I was into art photography and wanted him to model for me. He wasn't particularly surprised or confused, and didn't ask for any more details; he accepted my invitation immediately, and seemed quite relaxed. He kept talking all the time, so I didn't have to keep up the conversation, as I do in most cases. He told me his name was Nenad, he was seventeen and born in Plitvice in Croatia, where his parents still lived. He was studying in Belgrade at the high school of biology. He lived with his uncle, though his parents owned a house here too. His father manages a private restaurant and owns a cafe in Plitvice, and his mother is a shop assistant. He is an only child.

He still kept talking when we got to my place. His father is thirty-seven (two years younger than me), tall, athletic physique, and weighs over a hundred kilos. A couple of years ago he was injured in a crash with a police car. It wasn't his fault, but he had several fractures, his diaphragm tore, his kidneys stopped functioning, etc. He was saved by treatment at the Army Hospital in Belgrade, where he stayed several months. He has a uncle in Frankfurt, who works at the American military base on steam-engines used for heating rocket hangars. He also has relatives in America. We talked as well about writing, prostitution, politics, and so on. I asked him about his sex life; he told me he had a girlfriend from Plitvice who was with him in Belgrade.

Since I was impatient to get things started, I showed him some magazines with nude art photos, which always serve as a good alibi and introduction to the 'photo session'. I told him this was exactly the kind of photograph I wanted to shoot. To justify my interest in male nudes I told him I was bisexual, equally attracted by female and male bodies (I always have to explain the word 'bisexual' as many people don't know). I said that I wanted to reveal in my photos the beauty and erotic dimension of the male body, because photography of this type is neglected in our country.

He agreed with my cheap theories. I always use a verbal introduction that reveals my secret slowly, to give my victim

around with my hand. I was sorry that he came so quickly. Afterwards we went on talking as if nothing had happened; we didn't mention sex at all. I was very talkative, as I generally am at that stage, to prevent him thinking too much about what had happened; he still might have reacted violently. But he showed no sign of repentance or intolerance. We had a shower together, and I even soaped his back and his arse. We put on our clothes in a hurry — I wanted him out of my flat as soon as possible; you never know what might happen.

When I was giving him a ride back to Republic Square, where his bus stop was, I asked him if he was angry about what had happened. He said politely that he wasn't. He even said he'd had sex with a friend at a youth camp; they just caressed and masturbated each other. Finally, he said he didn't care if he was with a man or a woman. I was surprised and glad to hear he thought that way. The boy had progressive opinions, which is untypical of people of his age here. After that, I decided to give him my phone number, quite unusual for me, and he put it down on a matchbox. I hoped he wouldn't lose it and that he would call me. While we were driving, he took the half-bar of chocolate out of his bag and offered it to me. I took some of it and laughed; he ate the rest on the way. I left him in front of the Hotel Majestic. We waved to each other; I adored him at that moment.

December 17th, 1988

Sex, Lies and Politics

The well-known 'Martinović Affair' caused many reactions in our press. The basic question in it is whether Martinović, a Serb, pushed a bottle up his own arse during masturbation, or whether it was done by two unknown Albanian separatists. It happened in a meadow outside a village in Kosovo. Of course, many Serbs said it was out of the question that a Serb would want to stick a bottle up his arse, therefore it must have been done by Albanians. As opposed to that the federal police claimed, to prevent any nationalist incident, that Martinović did it to himself. By the way, the bottle was thrust with such force that it broke inside the poor guy and injured his anus; it is highly unlikely that anyone would have deliberately injured themselves so badly. I read in the last issue of *Nin* that Stane Dolanc, a Slovene and former head of Interior Security (the secret police, SDB), is to be blamed for covering up the truth of the case.

Dolanc introduced the version according to which Martinović was the one who injured himself whilst masturbating with the bottle up his arse. Thus the man who in fact was the victim of cruel violence was in addition publicly disgraced for being a homosexual masturbating with a bottle. All this was done for political reasons and higher national interests (preserving brotherhood among nationalities). The doctors who examined him said that even a layman could see how absurd was the claim that Martinović inserted a half-litre bottle eighteen centimetres into his own anus. The bottle was six and a half centimetres wide so it would have been impossible to use it for masturbation. Martinović said that inspectors of the federal police threatened to torture him with electricity unless he said his injuries were self-inflicted. The police said they knew of previous cases. This obscure political-criminal-sexual offence raises many questions.

First, why did these Albanians, who actually did it, decide to injure Martinović in that particular way? Why stab him in the anus with a glass bottle? Their original intention must have been not only to injure him physically but also to humiliate and disgrace him. In their eyes, their victim was a symbol of their fiercest enemy, so they wanted to dishonour him in the worst possible way, to unman him and to destroy his masculine pride. Of course that raises the question why it is such a disgrace for a man when something or somebody penetrates his anus — in this case a bottle substituting for an Albanian cock. Why did those Albanians find a triumphal revenge in that symbolic anal rape and why again did so many Serbs find it to be such an unbearable humiliation, one which called for vengeance against Albanians? A whole essay could be written on that question.

Another question was why the federal police made up the version about Martinović injuring himself? As I mentioned already, the main reason was probably to prevent the spread of hatred between the Serb and Albanian communities in Kosovo; the situation there had been delicate and extremely tense for a long time. If that was their goal then it was quite reasonable and normal. But it was horrible that a man who already was a victim of assault, was also the person who was unscrupulously sacrificed and additionally disgraced for some higher political and national interest. That was done in the old communist-totalitarian tradition according to which the dignity, destiny and life of an individual means absolutely nothing when it comes to so-called higher national interest. At the same time, the Serb nationalists did their best to prove that Martinović was actually raped, because such a thing would help their plans for abolishing the autonomy of Kosovo, and for a greater presence of the army and police forces in the province. They did not care about the fate of the man either; for them too, his misfortune was just an instrument for their political goals and a means to whip up Serb nationalism.

I wonder whether the whole affair would have had such dimensions if the criminals had simply beaten Martinović up, or cut off his ear. I don't believe it would. I think that the rape with the bottle was the key point in it all. Such an act of humiliation is the worst possible thing that can happen to a man according to the Serbian-Orthodox patriarchal view of virility, and those Albanians, apparently, knew this. Besides, it seems to me that Serbs are more afraid of homosexuality that other people. The peoples of western and central Europe who enjoy a higher level of culture and civilisation than we do, accept homosexuality more and more as a manifestation of human nature, which is bisexual in its essence. The nations in the south of Europe, and especially Greeks (our Orthodox brothers) already have a long tradition of bisexual behaviour. They did not need Weininger, Freud, Marcuse and others to tell them that man is a bisexual being, they have known this since ancient times. Lastly, Muslims all over the world, including Albanians, are prone to homosexuality — a fact confirmed not only by my own experience but also by social science. For all these peoples, man-to-man sexual intercourse is not so shocking a thing as it is to Serbs.

I have had several opportunities to meet very manly Albanians who had sex with women, but who during intercourse with me only wanted to take the 'passive' role. In their consciousness all this functioned perfectly logically and naturally — if they are with a woman they fuck, if with a man they are fucked. No complex, no feeling of guilt and no humiliation. For them it was purely a question of sexual pleasure and not a question about some symbolic 'unmanning' or 'desecration' of the sacrosanct male arsehole. Here in Serbia even homosexuals who like to be fucked do not want to admit it. Most of them are ashamed of it, so they try to hide it. Everybody pretends to be 'a great fucker', including gays and tough macho guys. We as a people are obsessed with our 'superior' masculinity and that is why the Martinović case became a major scandal and a disgrace for the nation.

December 18th, 1988

Dandy Quarrelsome Patients

Today's *Politika* published an article on people with AIDS. The woman journalist writing the report visited, together with a doctor, the sixth ward of the Infectious Diseases Clinic, where AIDS patients are treated. During her visit she talked with four drug addicts, two haemophiliacs and two bisexuals (a euphemism for homosexuals). When she deals with haemophiliacs the journalist is full of pity and sympathy for the "innocent and unfortunate victims of this cruel disease". She is much less compassionate towards the drug addicts, dealing out a great deal of moralistic criticism and describing one of the addicts as a "tall and handsome young man who could have been the pride of his generation". Lastly when talking about the homosexuals she comes out with all the usual prejudices between the lines:

"Only shadows remain of the dandy faces of two bisexuals in the next room. Neither of them allowed the the doctors to perform a lumbar puncture because they couldn't stand the pain... There was a homosexual who arrived from Germany with syphilis and tuberculosis. It was found that he was also infected with AIDS — a diagnosis he didn't believe. He walked along the corridors putting on airs, in his silk negligée, a discreet smell of men's perfume surrounding him. He was not part of the sad and despairing ambience of the ward. He returned to Germany in an ambulance and the trip was paid for by someone he had over there. Soon after he died."

There are many interesting statements in this short extract: a) homosexuals are 'dandy', which sounds a bit effeminate and humiliating. It turns out that only heterosexuals can be beautiful, well-behaved and 'real men'; b) homosexuals are cowards because they 'couldn't stand the pain', unlike normal straight men who are brave and really enjoy lumbar punctures; c) besides having AIDS homosexuals are infected with all sorts of other diseases — syphilis, tuberculosis, etc.; d) they are quarrelsome and like to put on airs; e) they like to adorn themselves like women with silk negligées, etc. which is not typical of a Balkan macho guy; f) they like to wear expensive perfumes too much, which in these parts is considered a feminine quality. Our real man should smell of sweat and tobacco — sometimes allowed to use a bit of 'Pitralon', 'Brion' or some other cheap after-shave lotion with a discerning smell; g) lastly, homosexuals are immoral and prostitute themselves to decadent westerners. That message is conveyed by the fact that the guy's ambulance transfer was paid for by somebody else. The intelligent reader will easily understand the person in question is a rich old German that our quarrelsome dandy lived with. The sick person therefore got what he deserved: death. Not only was he a faggot, but — horror of horrors — he actually left for Germany, the traditional enemy of Serbia, and got involved with a German pervert.

February 13th, 1989

A Good Husband and Father

I had a date with Boban, the guy I met the other day, to meet with him in front of the American Centre Library at half past four. I waited for him for almost a quarter of an hour after the appointed time, but he didn't show up. I started walking towards Staklenac, an underground pedestrian passage where there are notorious public toilets, as well as several shops and a pizza parlour. I was feeling quite disappointed, but met Boban on the way, which surprised me and cheered me up. He said he'd been waiting for me in the wrong place, near the fountain in front of the cinema Jadran. It was pure luck that we met, and we went over to my place.

On arrival I started a conversation to make him relax because I felt he was pretty nervous. He sipped juice and I had tea. He told me that he was in the second grade of the Nikola Testa secondary technical school. He was from Smederevo, and his parents also lived there. His father was an electrician and his mother, a housewife. He lived with his aunt in Belgrade. His aunt was very nice. He was into sports, especially full-contact I don't know exactly what that is but I suppose it is some sort of martial art — ninja style. He probably said that to impress me because he may have been a bit afraid of me.

As the conversation didn't ease his tension I decided not to lose valuable time but to start our photo session immediately. First, I took a couple of shots of his head in order to mask my real intentions. I then told him to remove his T-shirt. He had a smooth, hairless chest perhaps a bit too broad for his height. He took off his trousers when told to do so. But when told to remove his underpants he grumbled and hesitated. I finally persuaded him to do so. I touched and caressed him every time I repositioned him, making it seem accidental. Unfortunately, he remained distracted and his small cock refused to wake up. I even tried to excite it, telling him that his cock should appear bigger in photographs. This didn't help and his cock refused to become erect. As he was still nervous and sombre, I decided that it was not the right moment for the realisation of my plan. I did not push it any more, I stopped shooting and suggested we went out, which he accepted with visible relief. I gave him a lift downtown.

★★★

Angry because of my failure, I took a stroll down Prince Mihajlo Street, finishing it in Staklenac where I intended to look for an opportunity for consolation. On Terazije Street I noticed a tall handsome guy wearing a leather jacket and carrying a plastic bag standing in front of the Rad bookshop. He looked quite familiar to me. I couldn't remember where I met him, but then it came to me. His name was Fadil, and he was introduced to me once in Milija's place. We were supposed to have sex, but I wasn't free that day. I approached him and shook hands with him, perhaps a little too cordially. He didn't recognise me for a moment. I asked him where he was going and he told me he had visited a friend in order to borrow some money because he was flat broke and was now on his way to get something to eat. He had to hurry home because his wife and child were waiting for him. The child was hungry and there was nothing to eat in the house. I invited him over to my place saying I would give him a lift home later.

He thought for a moment and then said yes. On our way he told me that he had been married now for four years and that he had an eighteen-month-old son. They lived in a small house — probably a shanty — given to him by his father in that part of the city around the hospital in Bežanijska Kosa. He had finished only his primary school and had never learnt a trade. He was of Bosnian origin, a Muslim to be more exact, but was born and raised in Zemun. He worked as a labourer in a paper mill until they fired him only a couple of days earlier. So he was trying hard to find a new job, anything would do — he was completely broke. When we got to my place I gave him some vodka (I did this on purpose as I wanted his mouth clean before he started kissing and licking me) and I drank some tea. We had a short formal talk and then went down to the main reason for his visit — I knew he was in a hurry. We lay on the couch kissing each other for a while before moving to the bed. He had a big handsome body. Unfortunately it was rather hairy and in the first phase of getting fat. He had the name Vesna tattooed on his upper right arm and an unintelligible design on his left, probably a dragon or something. He caressed me gently and sucked my cock. I caressed him too, squeezed his arse and now and then inserted my finger into his anus. He did not try to resist. I placed my cock between his legs. He probably expected me to fuck him but I did not want to take such a risk. I discharged when he was sucking my cock and rubbing my perineum. He swallowed my sperm but didn't orgasm himself. I quickly washed my cock and he washed his mouth out. We dressed in a hurry and I gave him a lift to his place just as I said I would.

He offered me a cup of coffee at his place but I wasn't in the mood to have a forced conversation constantly interrupted by his wife and the baby crying in the god-forsaken hole they lived in. I regretted my decision later, I could have visited him and seen his place. The whole story seemed very funny and queer — a husband goes out to borrow money to buy some food. On the way he meets a gay man, gives him a blow-job and nearly gets himself fucked for a mere two and a half million dinars. As if that wasn't enough, he moreover invites the homosexual to meet his wife and drink coffee at his place.

It is a pity I didn't have enough patience to wait for all the acts of this little play. If only some women knew what their macho husbands get up to! I again found great pleasure in the role of an avenger who allows bullies and macho men to give him blow-jobs or to be fucked for some money. So, I felt like I humiliated the man, a husband and a father, by letting him suck my cock and even gulp down my sperm. I know I am ridiculous with my ideas of the revenge I get on straight men, the establishment and the wider society. I sometimes wonder to what extent my sexual excitement results from some other non-sexual motivation.

February 21st, 1989

A Father and Son

I met a guy wearing a check jacket and jeans at the bus stop near Karadjordje Park. I did not like him particularly at first sight, but I noticed he liked me (which happens less and less as I get older). After a short chat, I invited him back to my place. However he said that he never went back to anyone's place on the same day they first met. I was unpleasantly surprised at his way of thinking. At his proposal we went for a walk. While we were walking towards Slavija, he talked about himself. He said he was twenty-three and was from Trebinje. He studied geology and was in the third year. He was after a high average grade but recently he'd not been doing so well. He lived in the 'Lola' students' dormitory and ate at students' restaurants. He seemed to be pretty shy, confused and constrained — a typical modest student who, after being brought up in traditional rural surroundings, comes to the big corrupt city. He had not rid himself of his provincial restraints and norms. I also had the impression that deep within him there was a feeling of guilt for being homosexual. Despite the fact that he obviously liked me he would not come to my apartment because that would have clashed with his principles, also perhaps because he was a little afraid of me, so he needed time to get to know me better.

After I spent a while trying hard to persuade him he finally agreed to go back with me. When we got there he refused any liquor and just drank strawberry juice. We continued talking — I led the conversation to make him more relaxed. I did not want to make love in haste with no words and without getting to know him better.

Amongst other things he told me that his father was homosexual. I was surprised, because it went against all my prejudices about the 'honest and traditional' provinces. At first I thought he was making the story up but later concluded from the impression his character had made on me that he was in fact telling the truth. It was only him in his family who was au fait with his father's gayness. His mother and sister were ignorant of this fact. His father also knew that he was gay though they never spoke about it. It was a painful subject for both of them and they had a tacit agreement never to mention it. Both of them were quite embarrassed. He told me that he avoided being in the house when his father was there. I said I could understand these feelings but that they were dreadful and absurd.

I recalled the relationship between Thomas Mann and his son Klaus. They were both homosexual and knew about each other's homosexuality. That caused difficulties in their case too, the father was embarrassed whenever he met his son and consequently was very cold towards him. Klaus seemed to suffer for this alienation from his father and for not being able to have an honest and more sincere relationship with him. In a society organised and ruled by heterosexuals, it is natural for children to assume their fathers must be heterosexual. Cases when the father of a family turns out to be gay are particularly scandalous and unexpected. It is quite natural to think that there are problems when a father is a homosexual and his son a heterosexual or the other way round. But one might also assume that the relationship between a gay father and his gay son would be as harmonious as if the two were heterosexuals. Nonetheless it does not seem to be the case, and the former kind of relationship is quite difficult, burdened with a feeling of guilt, self-discontent and even mutual intolerance. The reasons for this are probably to be found in the dominant homo-repressive culture.

It even seems to me that a father and son of whom one is a homosexual and the other is not get along much better than when they are both homosexual. Such cases also raise the question of the genetic predisposition of homosexuality — theories of which are still around though often refuted. Such father-son relationships should get more space in psychology and literature. I haven't read anything about this problem, except a few things explained by Klaus Mann in his diaries, *The Turning Point*.

We talked a bit more but the rest of the conversation was really quite boring. When I got fed up, I decided to make the first move because he obviously wasn't able to do that. He was stiff and clumsy, but we started having sex after a while. When we kissed I avoided touching his mouth with mine. I managed to take his trousers and underpants off although he defended himself like a virtuous girl who wanted to protect her chastity. It seemed that something was preventing him taking off his underpants. His cock was big enough but somewhat crooked. Perhaps that was what he was ashamed of. He kept taking up positions which made me believe he wanted me to fuck him up the arse. I didn't even think of doing that, although he said he'd only ever made love twice before and hoped he hadn't caught AIDS. When I suggested we move to the bed, he said he wanted to stop, but we continued after I asked him to. I masturbated whilst he was caressing my balls and eventually stained my T-shirt with my own sperm.

While I was having a shower he got dressed. He just had a cigarette and left. Before he left, I gave him my telephone number. I don't know why I did so because I had no interest in him whatsoever. He was quite boring and tiresome and the sex we had was also very bad.

March 5th, 1989

The Awl

The other day I met a long-haired youth I used to see quite often and with whom I'd made love a couple of times. I met him in Staklenac. He hadn't had any homosexual experience before meeting me. We had sex twice; the first time we caressed, cuddled, kissed and sucked each other and the second time I fucked him. I didn't hear from him again, though I often saw him standing in front of the Zagreb restaurant with his mates — a group of dishevelled long-haired boys and girls wearing black leather jackets and black jeans. I later found out that this was a meeting place for drug users. Mostly he took no notice of me and when our eyes met he would simply nod. Occasionally we would stop to chat a little. On those occasions I always told him to get in touch with me hoping we'd have sex again. But he never did and so I gave up hope. Nevertheless when I met him the other day he was very talkative and friendly and he promised to call me. He did in fact call and so we made an appointment to meet in front of the Albanija building at seven o'clock.

I arrived a little early and he showed up soon after. He was wearing a cheap little blue cap with USA embroidered on the front and a small metal cross pinned to it. He was also wearing white sneakers — always a turn-on for me. He was a bit confused and disappointed that I'd turned up so early — something I found rather strange. We got into my car and made for my apartment. I asked him various questions en route trying to keep the conversation going — I could sense that he was tense and nervous. Something was wrong with him.

When we arrived at my flat he became even more nervous. First he went into the bathroom, then he paced around the room and looked at the bookshelves, stared out of the window, followed me into the kitchen when I wanted to pour drinks, etc. He was unable to stay in one place and was behaving like a caged lion. His nervous walking made me suspicious and irritable. I had this premonition that he wanted something from me. At the moment when I went to my desk to get something he approached me from the side and started hitting me in the back. I pushed him away and ran to the corridor. He rushed towards me and we started wrestling, with him hitting me all the time. He knocked me to the floor where we went on wrestling. He was much stronger and more skilful so he managed to pin me to the floor and sat on my chest. He said he would kill me unless I gave him some money. I said as calmly as I could in the circumstances that he would kill nobody and that I would give him some money, and that he could have asked for it without all this fuss. He calmed down a little and I told him I had some money in the kitchen, so he allowed me to get up on my feet.

I took a bundle of banknotes from the pocket of my jacket, they were in five-thousand dinar notes totalling about four to five million dinars. At the same time I took the apartment keys and, anticipating something more, locked the flat from the inside and hid the keys in a kitchen drawer. This was a mistake. I hardly knew what I was doing, as I had cut off my escape route and found myself trapped. I gave him the money, and while he was counting it in the room, I quickly unlocked the main door and went out into the hall. I immediately rang my neighbour's doorbell — just in case!

He ran out furiously after me and asked me what I was doing — what a silly question! I told him to beat it at once and to leave me alone. Seeing that the situation was turning in my favour he took his jacket and shoes and rushed down the stairs.

As soon as he'd gone I went back into my flat and felt this bad pain in my back. I touched the painful bit and felt something hard and cold. Looking in a mirror I noticed that a metal awl without its handle was actually sticking out of my back. I tried to pull it out but couldn't quite get a grip. After several attempts I finally found the right angle and pulled it out. I took off my shirt and could see that my underwear was completely covered in blood. I had four or five quite shallow stab wounds and bruises and a very deep wound where the awl had been.

On top of all this I was experiencing severe chest pains and was having difficulty breathing — probably because he'd been sitting on my chest with all his weight.

I quickly changed my clothes, took my health insurance papers, went down to my car and drove furiously to a hospital — in fact a first-aid station. They treated my wounds rather quickly. They gave me an anti-tetanus jab, disinfected the wounds and X-rayed my chest. A surgeon told me that no bones were broken, that my lungs were okay and that there were no internal injuries. He told me that the chest pains and the breathing difficulties would soon cease. He told me just to take some pain-killers and nothing else. Another unpleasant surprise awaited me on the way out — a uniformed cop wanting a statement (hospitals are obliged to call the police in such cases). I did not dare say what actually happened (and I did not in fact want to), because it would reveal the homosexual background of the incident. I quickly made up some story for the police. I told him I went out for a stroll on the quay in front of my block when all of a sudden I was attacked by two guys. They stabbed me, knocked me down and took my money. Soon, a patrol car drove up with three inspectors in mufti and I had to repeat the same story. It was not enough for them, so they asked me to take them to the place where it all happened. I drove my car and they followed in theirs. I could hardly drive because of the pain.

When we arrived I still did not know which place to show them as the place of the assault. I walked down the quay slowly — I told them I was in great pain — looking around nervously and thinking which place to choose. I chose the darkest place near an old barge. Then they took photographs of the place with a camera equipped with an extremely strong flash. Later, we went to the municipal police precinct on 29th November Street so that I could make a statement. When I was leaving they gave me the phone number of a certain Inspector Cekić who was in charge of such cases and whom I called the next day.

I went to Marko directly from the precinct. I told him about the whole thing. The guy could have killed me if the handle had not come off the awl, leaving it stuck in my back. I was also lucky that he stabbed me in the back rather than in my neck, heart or stomach — which would have been much more dangerous and perhaps fatal. I had the impression that my assailant was probably a junkie who needed money at whatever cost. Marko was shocked. He gave me some tranquillisers, pain-killers and tea. I was afraid to go back home alone, because there was a danger that the guy would return with his gang to attack me further. Marko went with me to cheer me up. We took his father's gun, an old Luger, in order to protect ourselves — the gun was however quite empty. Everything went well, nobody was waiting for us there. I watched a film based on a novel by Agatha Christie, while Marko leafed through old porno mags. I could not sleep that night because of the pains in my chest and back.

★★★

March 6th, 1989

I had to go to the faculty this morning to attend an exam. I could hardly move because of the pains. Everyone noticed my strange posture and my stiff way of walking. I told Nena and Mira in confidence about what had happened. They were shocked and scolded me for being irresponsible and for doing such silly things. I kept analysing the whole event in my head. My intuition kept telling me from the moment when we met that something was wrong and that something bad was going to happen. A black cat crossed my path both when I left my apartment and when I returned — and people say you should not be superstitious! His behaviour revealed something dangerous and threatening. I always make mistakes and repent when I do not listen to my intuition. When I think of the things that might have happened to me I shudder. He could have pierced my eye, throat, my neck artery, temple or heart with the awl he stabbed me in the back with. Fortunately it must have stuck between my ribs so he couldn't use it any further — he must have held just the plastic handle. He could have mutilated, crippled or even killed me. The police would have found my body in a pool of blood, and they would probably never have caught the murderer, because nobody saw me enter the flat with him. He would remain free and unpunished.

That was already the fourth or fifth time I've been physically assaulted and wounded. This time, however, I was closest to death. I was quite fortunate, I suppose. It seems that God is still helping me — they say that God helps the mad and the drunk, but it seems he also protects gays. I must go to a church and light a candle. I think of this as the beginning of a new life, given to me as a present — as another chance given me by the Almighty and also as the last warning to change my dangerous way of living. When I reflect on the incident, the boy did look like a frenzied junkie who desperately needed money for his dope. If it hadn't happened I would have had sex with him and possibly have caught AIDS — most drug addicts in Belgrade are infected. In fact maybe I eluded a much worse evil than the one I experienced. I should find some kind of moral in all this. From now on I will have to take more care about what I do and who I invite back to my home. Maybe I should even quit this risky and promiscuous way of life based on sex as the meaning of life. I must dedicate myself to a greater extent to my work, reading, writing, meeting friends, politics and other sorts of non-sexual activities and amusements. Let's just wait and see!

May 14th, 1989

The Taxi-Driver Murderer

Milija told me that little Dejan, whom I'd had sex with before my trip to China, was arrested. He was accused of murdering a taxi driver in Block 45 in Novi Beograd. Milija also showed me an article in *Politika*, where they published only Dejan's initials as he was still a minor at the time — only seventeen. He was arrested on the same day we'd had sex, which means that he'd killed the taxi driver just a couple of days earlier. He'd stabbed the driver several times and the stab in the heart proved fatal. He was sitting in Moskva cafe with Beli when the police came and picked them both up. That same evening I was also there sitting with Zoran and Giga, but I couldn't make out what was going on because we were at opposite sides and the arrests were made very quietly and discreetly.

I had no idea that I'd had sex with a murderer. The hands which had caressed me had stabbed that taxi driver's body. They could have killed me too. The mouth of that criminal had sucked my cock so nicely. I found it very exciting and erotic. It has been clear to me for a long time that the context in which sex takes place is more important than the sex itself. I like to make love in peculiar places, in a dangerous situation, and most of all with heterosexual men who've had no experience of male sex before. Sometimes I scold myself for my superficiality which makes me find the meaning of life in a cumulation of exciting events and adventures, and not in deep emotions, interests or spiritual values.

May 21st, 1989

President of Yugoslavia

Ever since a Slovene, Janez Drnovšek, became the president of Yugoslavia, there have been rumours that he is a homosexual. Serb politicians find these rumours useful since they compromise the Slovenian liberal and secessionist policy. In a mockingly intoned report, the Youth Radio Station B-92 said that Janez Drnovšek was the president of the committee of the organisation of the international congress of homosexuals in Ljubljana before he became President of the Republic. In gay circles in Belgrade there is a story that he was a regular visitor to gay bars and saunas in London, where he worked as a counsellor at our embassy. The rumours say further that he gave blow jobs there in dark rooms and that he may have even contracted AIDS there. If that is all true, not only does Yugoslavia have a gay president for the first time in its history, but one possibly infected with HIV.

The media under the control of the government do not yet openly attack him. Allusions and attacks are left to the yellow press and the spreading of false rumours. In that context there is a very 'nice' joke going the rounds in Belgrade, in the form of a short dialogue between the President of Serbia, Slobodan Miloševic, and the President of Yugoslavia, Janez Drnovšek.

Milošević: When are you going to give us the factories you moved from Serbia to Slovenia after the war?

Drnovšek: We won't give you a fuck!

Milošević: We won't ask for that much. We don't want to take cocks out of your mouths.

The Serb people like the joke quite a lot, in which the Serbian president wins as a witty, wise and manly protagonist in a verbal duel with a Slovene faggot, Drnovšek, who sticks other people's dicks in his mouth.

Everybody's saying that Drnovšek is ugly, bald, badly dressed, etc. Almost no one says that we have a president with a PhD in economics, a brilliant expert with many published works, a man who speaks four foreign languages and so on. Our public care more about the fact that he is not married at the age of forty and are happier to deal with what he did in London bars. We don't mind half-literate politicians who cannot string a sentence together, who cannot speak a single foreign language, who wear chequered suits with multicoloured ties tied in big knots, but we do mind gay politicians, no matter how educated and capable they might be. To tell the truth, it is a problem not only in our country, in most others the situation is similar. Homosexuals can't attain or maintain high political positions. Of course, there are a few exceptions — our president is, so it seems, a proof of this.

September 6th, 1989

A Clown on a Camel

I bumped into Dejan on Prince Mihajlo Street, a tall blond guy with a big dick, whom Sava and I met on the beach on Ada Island last summer. He was licking an ice-cream. He offered me a lick, which I refused for hygienic reasons. He suggested we went to see *Rambo II* showing at the 20th October cinema. I didn't feel like watching the film at all, but he was so pushy that I had to go with him. In fact, I hoped I would be able to wank off with him in the dark. I was too scared to take him back to my place because he could be dangerous.

We sat in the back row. As soon as the lights went off I started touching him. While he was watching the film, jumping up, shouting loud remarks and cheering Rambo, I concentrated on his cock. I put my hand inside his tracksuit pants, played with his cock, caressed it, squeezed it. It was the biggest and most beautiful dick I'd had in a long while. Long, fleshy, smooth, warm. He wasn't lying when he said it was twenty-four centimetres when erect. He got a hard-on in my hand, then it became softer, then hard again and so on, like a strange animal which constantly changed its size and texture. During the whole film, this strange metamorphosis of his dick went on and on. I enjoyed the game. From time to time he'd stroke my right hand which was responsible for waking up his animal. I took this an encouragement and a token of thanks.

★★★

After the film, I had a short walk and then went to the square in front of the National Theatre, to see our rulers and the leaders of the Non-Aligned countries gather for a gala performance on the occasion of the closing night of their meeting in Belgrade. Most dignitaries swept up in black Mercedes. To my surprise, of all the Yugoslav politicians, President Drnovšek got the loudest applause, despite him being a Slovene and a reputed homosexual. Of all foreign statespersons the loudest applause was for Sanjay Gandhi, the Indian prime minister, probably because everyone in the crowd knew of him, whereas other guests were much less famous.

The main reason for my presence was to see Ghadafi. He took three camels and a Bedouin tent to Belgrade. The tent was raised in the grounds of the Libyan embassy and he slept in it. He said he would come to the theatre riding a camel. I was waiting to see this. Unfortunately, the 'enfant terrible' of the so-called Non-Aligned movement did not show up. He was probably angry because of something or another and left before time. It's a pity! I stood in front of the theatre for more than an hour, watching leaders of the Non-Aligned world showing off in their black suits and tailcoats decorated with their medals. Some of them wore general's or marshal's uniforms. They looked pathetic. While I was watching the scene, I felt something hard against my arse. I saw a handsome Arab with a moustache standing behind me, maybe a member of the security team of some dictator. He pressed his cock against my arse, and I of course didn't move or complain. I felt sorry when the crowd dispersed.

December 5th, 1989

A Special Kind of Blood

The last number of the *Književne Novine* contains an interview with Emire Kusturica, a famous Bosnian film director, in which he says that when making his film *Time of the Gypsies* he found out that Gypsies, as a hot-tempered nomadic people, have a higher body temperature than people with permanent residence. According to Kusturica, there are other groups who also have this special kind of blood — groups such as homosexuals and TB patients, where the body temperature is a constant 37.1°C.

I have heard many stupid things about homosexuals in my life, but this is the first time I heard we have a higher body temperature. I can assure Mr Kusturica that I do not have a higher body temperature than is usual except of course when I catch flu or some other infection. In order to find an answer to this 'important' question and to test this 'serious scientific hypothesis', I suggest we carry out a comparative study with a group of heterosexuals on one side and a group of homosexuals on the other. Repeat it with Gypsies and non-Gypsies too. Doctors could check body temperatures of members of both groups regularly, three times a day during the period of a week for instance. I say that there would be no difference in body temperature between members of the different groups and propose a bet with Kusturica: if what I say proves to be true then let him give me the royalties he received for his films and if it turns out that his theory is true, I will give him the copyright on all the books I have written so far and those I may write in the future.

December 17th, 1989

Russian Sexual Culture

I hung around the railway station platforms hoping to pick someone up. I saw an extremely handsome dark-haired boy sitting on the stairs in front of the waiting-room having a nap. He wore a blue marine coat with brass buttons, stone-washed jeans and a pair of black laced boots. He had a small earring in his left ear. Those clothes made him seem a bit extravagant to me.

I asked him for the time, not having anything particular in mind. He jumped up and his gesticulation showed he could not understand me. It turned out that he came from the Soviet Union. Fortunately he spoke a little English so we were able to communicate. I invited him for a drink. He accepted the invite but first he went back into the waiting-room to tell his friends he was going to be absent for a bit. We went to the station restaurant and picked an outside table as the weather was lovely. I had a coke and he a large mug of beer. We talked for more than an hour. I was unable to understand half the things he said, partly because of his broken English and partly because I was so fascinated by his beauty and was scheming how to get him into bed.

In short he told me his name was Denis and that he was Ukrainian from Kiev though born in Odessa. He studied chemistry in Moscow. He was also in the army, the marine infantry stationed on the Black Sea — a bit like the US Marines. Of course that particularly turned me on. His father was a manager in a Soviet-German company and his brother of twenty-one had been killed in Afghanistan. (I'd already met a number of Russians who told me some of their relatives were shot in Afghanistan, but I never knew whether they were telling me the truth or making up stories so as to be more interesting to foreigners).

When I got tired of chatting in the restaurant, and knowing that Russians love to drink, I invited him back for a drink, porno movies and further conversation. In my apartment we drank steadily, I kept filling his glass up with spirits as part of my devilish scheme. He drank more than half a bottle of a cheap domestic brandy, while I just sipped a Martini. We talked about various things. He told me he would like to emigrate to America when he graduates — a typical dream of Russians and other Eastern Europeans. I tried constantly to start a conversation about sex. He complained that people in the Soviet Union were not free enough on the sexual front and did not have a developed 'sexual culture' — whatever that means. However, I grabbed this opportunity to demonstrate 'sexual culture' to him, so I told him quite coldly that I was bisexual. He reacted in the same way as if I'd told him I was a poet, with a sort of awe and respect. I asked him if he'd like to see a bisexual movie and he accepted. I then told him to go take a shower, which after a bit of protest he did.

While he was in the shower I stripped to my underwear, went to bed and put on a porno. He came out wearing my striped bathrobe and pants and sat on the bed beside me. He continued drinking, fascinated by what he was seeing on the TV. We were silently watching the movie for about ten minutes and then he lay down revealing his cock which was already extremely hard. I started tenderly caressing his thighs, fascinated by his wonderful hairless body. I caressed his cock under the pants, then took it out and held it firmly in my hand admiring its size. I stooped down and started sucking it eagerly. At that moment he went out of his mind. He started sucking me wildly. We kissed and fucked each other violently. Afterwards he told me it was the first time in his life that he'd made love with a man. As he was tired of travelling he soon fell asleep, partly a result of the alcohol he'd consumed and the outrageous sex we'd enjoyed. I was unable to sleep, so watched CNN all night. I could hardly wake him the next morning — he had to be at the station by seven to meet up with his companions. Before we left the flat we had a quickie. It was not so exciting as the previous night because I'm not that keen on sex in the morning. He sucked my cock and licked up my sperm. He was obviously not afraid or aware of the risk of AIDS. We exchanged addresses, he told me that he'd be back in Belgrade in March to buy a second-hand Lada.

II : 1991—1993
WAR AND DISASTER

February 17th, 1991

Material Fatigue

I neglected my diary for quite a long time again. A lot of things have happened, more of them around me than to me, but I was too lazy to write them down. The main event was the opposition demonstration that took place in the Square of the Republic on March 9th last year, and the students' demonstrations in Terazije. I saw quite a few gay people among the demonstrators. Arkadia — the newly formed illegal gay organisation — issued a proclamation in support of the demonstration on behalf of homosexuals, which was read out on the student radio station B-92 and Radio Pančevo. Among other things many of the demonstrators shouted "Sloba-Saddam" and "Sloba is a faggot", so Arkadia made a protest demanding that the word 'faggot' not be connected with the name of the president.

There were many casualties at the demonstrations, two dead and several beaten up. The police threw tear gas at people and used rubber bullets, occasionally even real ones. The uncle of one of my friends had his eye smashed in and a student of mine, one of the demonstration's leaders, had his jaw smashed and lost almost all his upper teeth. My friend Marko made a last-minute dash from the raging police who beat anyone they managed to catch. The police displayed an unprecedented degree of brutality. I have no doubt that it was done with permission from the top.

I'm breathing heavily and I can't get enough air, it's a consequence of my lowered lung capacity. I'm afraid I will die soon. I have no other interest but sex. Most of all I pick up young Romanians who hang around the railway station. I make love with them for a hundred dinars. Most of them are cold and unskilled at homosexual love-making so they don't give me much pleasure. Besides which they are often dirty and smelly, which disgusts me.

My relationship with Alex is going through a crisis. We get to see and hear from each other less and less frequently. Our love-making is also getting worse, as if there is a fatigue in the material it is made of. Bearing in mind that sex is the main thing in our relationship I can't see it lasting much longer. We are often afraid of being alone together because we don't have anything to talk about. Therefore we are always trying to keep someone else company.

Dad is getting worse, he had two heart attacks in the last ten days, so we had to call an ambulance. The doctor said that his heart is very weak and only functions with twenty per cent capacity. Also his colon cancer has spread to his liver and pancreas. Luckily he feels no pain yet and remains clear-headed and completely aware of the situation. He doesn't want to go into hospital but wants to die at home, surrounded by his family, not by doctors and nurses. I understand him thoroughly and suppose I'd want the same if I were in his shoes. My problem is that I'll probably have no one around me at my dying hour.

Besides laziness, the reason I haven't kept my diary these days has been that making records of everyday events leaves me even more depressed. I can hardly make it through the day, and when I put events down on paper I go through them once again in my mind and feel disgusted with myself. Writing about a life like mine is pure masochism. I'm sick of dealing with myself all the time. My diary just makes me conscious of my poor and unsuccessful existence. That's the real reason why I stopped writing. I wanted to avoid dealing with myself twice — once in real life and then again on paper. I tried to occupy my mind with other things so as to divert my attention from myself. I failed. The articles I am writing, numerous books I started to read without the intention of finishing, films on video, imitations of friendships — none were enough to absorb me and divert my attention. Most of the time I sit in my corner in front of the TV, often making breaks in which I muse or take naps. I always hope the phone will ring and that it will be someone with a sexual offer.

October 1st, 1991

Mobilisation

I am more and more afraid that there will be a war between Serbia and Croatia. I always thought they would not mobilise me as I have never been in the army because I had hepatitis. I felt very safe and war seemed only a very slight possibility. But now there are rumours that there will be a general mobilisation which means nobody will be able to escape being called up, not even those like myself who've never been in the army because of illness.

Now I am in a panic about it. I can see myself on the front line, surrounded by dirty soldiers with beards, thirsting for blood and robbery, protected by the slogan 'Anything for the protection of Serb homes'. I think they would immediately see that I was not one of them, that I do not see patriotism and national interest with their eyes, and that I do not hate Croats or Muslims. That would be enough for them to harass or even kill me. Moreover, if they found out I was gay, they would probably humiliate me, molest and mock me. Even if I managed to imitate their model of patriotism, there would still be the risk of getting wounded. I could lose an arm, a leg, eyes, a part of my face, etc. which all seems more horrifying than actual death. Finally, I would be most scared if I were to be captured by Croats (HOS or ZNG troops). They would probably torture me until I died. I always have in mind horrible pictures of captives tortured on both sides in war: cutting off arms or legs with a power saw, taking out eyes or tongue, being 'barbecued' and ripped, taking out the heart, cutting off genitals, slitting throats, etc. How does one feel when you see the executioner approaching with a power saw to cut off your legs or with a knife to cut out your eyes. Such a horror is inconceivable, yet I am constantly haunted by such images. My worst nightmare is the moment of being approached by my executioner.

With all this in mind, I am trying to make a scheme which would save me in case they send me an 'invite' for the war. For example, I could have my hernia operated on and thus, at least temporarily, postpone going away to fight; I could take leave and flee the country like so many young people have done already; I could ignore the call-up and go to jail (I would at least stay alive and have sex in jail); take an AIDS test and, if I was positive (God forbid), they'd probably spare me; find connections and protection in order to get myself into the Civil Defence Organisation or into the rear lines and thus survive this war; or flee to a high mountain covered with dense forests and live there as a recluse; last, I could go for a sex change.

October 28th, 1991

A Manly Genital People

According to the *Vreme* magazine, Dr Jovan Rašković, a psychiatrist and the former leader of Serbs in Croatia, said in an interview he gave on Studio B television: "It is only gays who have nothing against Serbia now." I really wonder what he meant. Are gays on the side of the Serbs because they are so handsome and manly that we simply can not resist them? That is in harmony with the famous statement made by the intellectual snob and ultra-rightist ideologist Dragoš Kalajić. The story has it that a lady asked him at a party in Rome whether it was true that Serbs raped Muslim women, and Kalajić answered: "My dear lady, Serbs are so manly that they don't have to rape anyone, women just fall into their arms." Later, Kalajić repeated his witty answer to the press. I haven't heard anything more repulsive and cynical. So, Muslim women look forward to being captured and raped by irrestistible Serb warriors. After what Rašković had to say it seems that gays have the same opinion as Muslim women.

Another possibility is that Rašković meant that everybody has fled the country except the worst stratum, gays. The word 'gays' was used here as an appropriate synonym for social scum, rabble, the same as drug addicts, prostitutes, alcoholics, thieves and so on. I think he was wrong. First, I do not believe "it is only gays who have nothing against Serbia" (or the actual Serbian regime). Neither gays from abroad, nor the ones from the country (and especially not them) can be on the side of the regime which gives the police and gangs enough power to beat them, humiliate them and to rob them. I don't believe that drug-addicts and alcoholics support the regime either (spirits and alcohol are more and more expensive, while people have less and less money), or prostitutes who are persecuted by the police, exploited by their pimps, while their wages go down because their potential customers get poorer every day. The only social group which has enough reason to support the regime consists of thieves, gangsters and the mafia, the carriers of organised crime. They have become so rich during the war through robberies, cheating and various machinations that they have become a new elite overnight. They have great social power now and even occupy high social positions. Our country aptly illustrates the 'South American syndrome' where corrupted politicians are supported by the rich mafia.

It is interesting that Dr Rašković seems so obsessed with homosexuality. He recently published a book where he divided Yugoslav men into several groups according to their sexuality: Croats belong to the 'castrated type', Muslims to the 'anal type' and Serbs, of course, to the 'genital type'. This case is another example of the mixing of sexuality with everyday politics. Rašković also says he is writing a book entitled *Protestantism and Homosexuality*. Having in mind our immediate environment, perhaps it would be better for him to deal with 'Orthodoxy and Homosexuality'.

November 11th, 1991

A Refugee from Croatia

While I was standing in front of the telephone booth at Staklenac I saw a nervous young man rush past the public toilet door, casting a furtive glance inside. It was clear to me that he was one of those guys who had heard about what went on in there but dared not stop and enter the toilet. I hurried up the stairs after him because such 'frightened' kids usually escape quickly. I caught up with him on Prince Mihajlo Street, in front of the Yugoplastika store. I approached him and asked where he was from. He seemed bewildered and I thought he would run away or reply angrily.

However he answered that he was from Bjelovar in Croatia. After breaking the ice, I went on with my questions. He replied with reserve, and I had the distinct impression that he didn't trust me. He told me that his father was an officer in the Yugoslav army and that he was still at the front in Croatia. He and his mother had fled from Bjelovar as it was no longer safe for them as Serbs. They had been living in Belgrade for five months or so. He had enrolled at the School of Tourism. He was born in Bjelovar and had spent all his life there before moving to Belgrade. He had many friends there and one never asked about other people's nationality. He said that he felt no hatred towards the Croats but did feel very sorry at having to leave his home town. He didn't much like Belgrade and the idea of being compelled to live here. He disliked many things, from the dirty streets and crowded buses to the impolite shop assistants as well as the general mentality of the place.

I concluded that this kid belonged to the group of completely 'Croatianised' urban Serbs who are despised by 'rural'

Serbs as traitors and perjoratively referred to as 'Crorbs'. They fully adopted the Croatian syndrome of being stuck-up. They look down on Serbs as their more primitive and retarded brothers in matters of culture and civilisation. The origins of this attitude lie in the fact that the Serbs were held under Turkish occupation for five hundred years, whereas Croats were a part of the well-developed Habsburg empire. On the other hand, the Serbs see the Croats as having been mere servants, stablemen and lackeys of the Habsburgs. This kid was a typical example of a Crorb. I already had the experience of meeting a couple of such refugees from Croatia. They didn't seem to like anything in Belgrade. They minded everything, the way tea was served in restaurants, that there were dried flowers in flower-pots, through to the stinking public toilets. They find it difficult to adjust to life here and the locals do not accept them easily. The gap between these 'Crorbs' and Serbs is quite logical, although they belong to one nation. According to their language and culture, these Croatian Serbs are actually much closer to the Croats than to the Serbs from Serbia — just as the Bosnian Serbs are in their mentality much closer to Bosnian Muslims.

For educated urban Serbs Orthodox religion and blood ties have a much lesser significance than language and culture. It is quite the opposite with uneducated peasants, to whom Orthodoxy and blood are more important than culture. Therefore it is quite clear why the main part of Serb resistance and secession is to be found in the villages of Croatia, and not in the cities. Having all that in mind, it is obvious why Serb refugees from Croatia cannot get used to life in Serbia. What do Serbs from Bjelovar or Osijek have in common with Serbs from Leskovac or Vranje, except the abstract sense of belonging to the same nation and confession? Everything that makes up concrete, everyday life separates them: language, customs, behaviour, habits, ways of dressing, attitudes, culture, etc. The illusion of 'blood ties' is broken by direct contact between 'Crorbs' and Serbs.

This all reminds me of the romantic illusion of many American black people that they are closer to Africans than to American whites. The only thing they have in common with Africans is their race and colour — everything else, the more important things in life, emphasise their difference. Proof of mutual intolerance between refugees and native inhabitants of Belgrade is getting more and more conspicuous, although the press hesitates to write about it and the state-run TV is completely silent. In fact, such intolerance is most obvious between Belgrade inhabitants and the refugees from Krajina and the Bosnian mountains. These refugees have brought with them to the city a new 'primitivism'. Their massive inflow is turning Belgrade into a Bosnian provincial town. They brought their crudeness, aggressiveness and intrusiveness, and their ugly dialect now dominates downtown Belgrade. All this causes hostility.

Anyway, I took the kid to my place. He had a tender boyish body with soft skin and no hair. Making love was exciting as usual. I licked his chest and belly, bit his neck and nipples. He licked me and sucked my cock. I could have fucked him and he tried hard to seduce me into it, but I held myself back from it. I didn't want to fuck him with my bare cock for reasons of health and I didn't want to go through the trouble of putting on a condom. There wasn't that much passion in it but it satisfied my criteria. Afterwards, I took him to the bus stop in direction of Bežanijska Kosa.

November 24th, 1991

A Self-Pitying Confession

I have been trying to formulate a couple of main things I should do in order to change my life, which has become senseless and monotonous — cruising every day in Staklenac and the railway station toilets. I feel I have to make a radical move. My main dilemma is whether or not I should go on obeying my sex drive, or try to become something I am not. Am I able to change my life at the age of forty-two to develop and reanimate my intellectual interests and creativity. All my so-called 'scientific work' has been uninteresting and performed without real enthusiasm. If I deceived others, I unfortunately was unable to deceive myself, unlike some of my colleagues who think they are serious scientific workers. Everything I have written is worth more or less nothing. There is hardly two or three per cent of my own authentic contribution, the rest being basically successful compilation from other authors. It is not really so strange since most university professors just copy others, the number of those who can write something completely original is very small.

So far, I have managed somehow to balance my pseudo-scientific work with my impulses. However, the older I get, the more obsessed with sex I become; rather than giving up sex gradually and turning more towards intellectual work, I'm becoming increasingly unable to read and write for long. Everything that isn't sex or an activity resulting directly in sex — hunting in toilets and parks — is, in my eyes, a complete waste of time. Sex has long been the essence of my life, my absolute point. Apart from sex there is nothing which really interests and absorbs me. I get totally fed up with things so quickly —

with television, books, friends, cafés, travelling... I am in a hurry even when making love with somebody — long drawn-out sex becomes boring and monotonous. When we finish sex I can't wait to get the person out of my flat — he becomes a bore to me. I don't know what to talk to him about — conversation becomes a real trial — as soon as my sexual interest in a person is over I'm not interested in him at all — I am cursed!

I simply am at a loss what to do — how to save myself. I no longer feel fit for living, at the same time I'm not yet prepared to die. I continue to have this crazy hope deep down that something will suddenly happen which will change my life; it is mainly the hope of experiencing a 'great love' which will bring me consolation and salvation. It's the only myth I believe in, the only self-deceit I allow myself. I still believe that love between two men is possible and that I could be one of the two. I believe it despite the fact that Forster thought such a love affair might be possible in literature but not in the real world. That's why he wrote *Maurice*.

December 26th, 1991

Tito and Warhol

Once, when Titoism was extremely popular, people chanted slogans for their beloved president enthusiastically: 'Long Live Tito!'; 'Tito, that means all of us!' Even after his death, the most popular slogan was the pathetic 'There's a Tito still after Tito!' But of course, not much of his work has remained after his death — neither socialism, nor Yugoslavia, nor the frequently preached brotherhood among nationalities. New nationalist leaders succeeded him and they destroyed Yugoslavia, cheered by misled people. Tito's cult was replaced by the cult of local leaders — Milošević in Serbia, Tudjman in Croatia, Izetbegović in Bosnia, and so on. As for Tito, he became posthumously 'the greatest enemy of the Serb people'. Now they call him 'Tito the faggot'. Here are two examples from newspapers:

"That faggot Broz said that peace must be attained by war, or something similar. This war will stop only when we reach the point which can satisfy us" (*Borba*, December 1st, 1991).

"Of all Yugoslavs, only Tito, with his 'ingenious' idea of brotherhood among peoples, deserves to be included in Warhol's constellation of transvestite and gay stars and other monsters and perverts"(*Osmica*, December 8th, 1991).

The former statement was made by a 21-year-old chetnik volunteer and the latter, which is even more confused, by a rightist intellectual snob and nationalist, the director Nebojša Pajkić. It fills me with disgust and scorn to hear those who once worshipped Tito say and write such things about him. I almost feel the need to defend him, although I hated him more than anyone else when he was in power. Of course, I didn't even dream at the time that much worse leaders would come to power, people I would hate even more than him. I am not one of those who are so upset by the present chaos, the civil war and the bloodshed, that they tell nostalgic stories about 'the good times under communism', when Tito was president and peace prevailed. I find Tito and communism responsible for what is going on, it was they who originally spread the germs of hatred. They managed to conceal and suppress all problems for forty years using force and propaganda, without giving any solutions. Those problems included smouldering nationalisms, which were suppressed by the meaningless concept of brotherhood. However, all this wouldn't have happened unless even worse politicians hadn't grabbed political power.

January 8th, 1992

The Empty Camera

As I could not pick anybody up in the places where gays gather, I decided to walk the streets and hunt heterosexuals. It's the kind of man-hunting which excites me most, because it is full of uncertainty and risk, and those forbidden fruits can be really sweet when picked. I am not always capable of this sort of activity because it takes a lot of energy, patience and strong concentration. I usually approach handsome guys who seem to be walking around with no particular destination and do not look dangerous. Usually I ask them the time, and then start a conversation or else beat a retreat, depending on their politeness, tone and depth of voice as well as body language. I can talk about the most banal things in order to see if the other guy wants to communicate. If it all works I invite him back to my place for a drink or to 'pose for my series of artistic photographs'. My impersonation of an artistic photographer is a risky technique, but it often produces good results.

If the 'victim' accepts my proposal I do not tell him I take nude photographs until we get in the car or even arrive at my apartment. It often turns out that they don't know what a nude photograph means, so I have to explain that I want to take photographs of them naked — at this point many of them chicken out and give up. If everything goes smoothly I offer the guest something to drink, talk with him for a while, show him some magazines with nude photographs — as if I did similar work — take my camera, adjust the flash and start taking pictures. Often I don't even have film in the camera. I'll start on his face, then I ask him to gradually strip off. When he is totally naked I help him to pose, touching his cock accidentally every now and then. Some of them get an erection and this is a good sign. I'll interrupt the session in order to cool down my flash. While waiting my model sits naked and I ask him if he'd like to watch some pornos. If he accepts I know that the situation is favourable because they usually get an erection and then I take the necessary steps. I put my hand on the victim's thighs, caress him, take his cock in my mouth...

★★★

I saw this handsome young lad, about nineteen, walking down the road apparently aimless, in front of Amfora on Terazije Street. I asked him the time and started a conversation. He looked a bit like an idler but he was very polite and answered my questions kindly. His name was Sasha and he lived in Cerak with his parents. He finished at secondary school doing chemistry but he was out of work and waiting for his army call-up. In his spare time he went out with his friends or played football, he used to do karate. He was bored, had no money and so just walked the streets killing time. I invited him over to my flat to watch some pornos. To my surprise he accepted.

When we arrived I gave him some apple juice. Our conversation was interrupted by long silences. Most of the time I asked him questions and gave comments about the political situation as we were watching the TV news — he gave short answers or said nothing. I wanted him to relax before we went on to pornos, but it wasn't easy as it was almost impossible to communicate with him. Before the news had finished I decided to put on the porno tape. I played a famous tape used for seducing naive heterosexuals. The tape begins with scenes of heterosexual love, then there are some bisexual combinations and, finally as a climax, homosexual scenes. Depending on the reaction of the person I either stop the tape at this point or let it roll further. Naturally I try to make myself useful at the same time.

In the beginning, during the heterosexual scenes, I gave excited comments on girls — their arses, tits, etc. I asked him if he liked big or small tits. He said medium size. I said that I liked small tits, which was closest to the truth that I don't like female breasts at all. I asked him about his own sexual life. He said that he'd fucked several girls but he couldn't remember the exact number. They also sucked his cock and he licked their cunts. He was too ashamed to give such answers freely and I had the impression he was making things up. I finally decided to take the crucial step. I started rubbing my own cock in my trousers until it became very hard. Then I took it out and started jerking off. At the same time I kept my eye on the guy to gauge his reaction. He started touching himself when he saw me doing so. I asked him if his cock was hard and he nodded confirmingly. I touched his zipper and felt that this was true. He opened his zip and I put in my hand in and grabbed his cock. At the same time he took hold of mine and we started masturbating each other. He then said that he was too hot and took all his clothes off. I followed. We embraced each other and kissed eagerly. We sucked each other's cock and licked each other, he even licked my arse. At the end I lubricated his anus and fucked him in all possible positions. He did not complain or say that I was hurting him.

I was very excited all the time. I enjoyed the whole thing, his beautiful young body, the sexual techniques and especially the fact that I considered him a heterosexual who was seduced by me just by accident. Before we went to bed I did not know what would happen, whether he would beat me or make love with me. Fortunately it turned out the latter. I gave him my telephone number but never saw him again.

January 13th, 1992

A Policeman-to-be

I spent the morning at the college. As the examination lasted longer than I thought I didn't go home for lunch. I ate ten *leskovacki cevap*'s, small meat rolls from the Question Mark café. Then I went to my aunt's for some cake. I spent the afternoon 'hunting' at Staklenac and in Zeleni Venac, without success. At about ten I went to Moskva and ordered tea with lemon. I was waiting for a familiar face to appear — or, even better, an unfamiliar one. A dark boy was sitting at a table near the bar, wearing a violet sweatshirt. He looked like a hooligan, but I remembered seeing him before sitting alone, and looking around. At that time he kept raising his eyes from the magazine he was reading and looking at people who came in. Our eyes met a couple of times, and after a while we were staring at each other.

This situation lasted for about ten minutes, then he went downstairs to the toilet. I waited for a bit then went after him inconspicuously. When I entered the toilet I saw him standing in a booth with the door half-open and masturbating, looking over his shoulder all the time. I didn't join him in the booth but went to a urinal and started wanking. He looked at me giving me a sign to join him. I whispered to him that it was dangerous to do it in the booth because the cleaning lady often came in to see what was going on, ever since a bomb was found there not long before. He accepted my explanation, and we went out one after the other. We both went to his table so as not to waste more time.

I noticed that he'd been reading the magazine *Vreme*. That was an encouraging sign. I concluded that the boy was probably smart and that we certainly shared similar political views.

He told me his name was Ivan and that he was twenty years old. He was in his second year at the college of mechanical engineering. He worked as a newspaper-seller on a Stampa stand in Slavija for a student organisation. He got the job through the influence of his uncle who was a section head in the city police. His uncle intended to find him a job as a policeman and get him promoted rapidly from constable to junior inspector. He was hesitating about it because he was frightened that they would examine his anus during a medical examination and discover that he liked getting fucked. I told him that such thoughts were absolutely unreasonable and ridiculous. First, I'd never heard that doctors examined the anuses of those applying for the police academy, and even if they did that was no way of discovering he was gay unless he was so fucked out that his anus looked like a volcano. He looked at me incredulously. I had the impression that I'd not convinced him at all. His naivety seemed tragicomic and likeable at the same time.

When we got back to my flat I made him some coffee. He asked me to play some porno videos for him. While we were watching we started making love and taking off our clothes piece by piece. When he was naked I saw he had a perfect body — exactly to my taste. It was slim, well-built, with well-defined muscles, but not too muscular like a body-builder's. His skin was soft and warm and hairless. I devoured his beautiful body with my eyes, delighting in it. I licked him from his neck down all over his chest and body, feeling under my tongue all those strong muscles under his skin. Then I put his huge cock in my mouth. Every part of him was first-class. Then we switched roles — he licked me all over and sucked my cock taking it all in his mouth. While we caressed I pushed my finger into his arse which he obviously liked. I decided to fuck him wearing a condom. I put lots of lubrication on him and massaged his anus slowly.

I started with one finger, but I was soon able to put three fingers in his hole. It seemed that I could have put my whole fist in if I'd been so inclined, he was so fucked out. I lost several erections before I managed to shove my dick in. His arsehole was so wide that it seemed like a tunnel, much too large for my cock. Because of that he didn't complain and felt no pain — he was used to much bigger rods than mine. I fucked him violently in various positions and he finally told me to fuck him while he was watching a porno. He lay on his stomach watching TV. I placed a big pillow under him so that his arse stuck right out. I fucked him for more than half an hour, while he stared at the screen enjoying himself. Meanwhile the condom broke so I continued screwing him with my bare cock. I discharged my cum inside him, but nothing seemed enough for him. He wanted me to fuck him some more. We had a short rest. As I couldn't get a hard-on he sucked my dick until it stiffened, then I gave him another half-hour fuck. He wanked himself off almost impaling himself on my cock.

After making love he stayed for a while to have a cigarette and a drink. He told me about his job, about the fact that he had a good salary because he sold his own stuff on the stand — cigarettes, hankies and other merchandise he bought from smugglers at low prices. The only problem was one of inspection. Once they caught him but his almighty uncle intervened and the whole thing was hushed up. He could not decide whether he should take the job with the police, bearing in mind the big money he earned on the street stand, in other words the loot. He said that the medical examination for the police job was on Wednesday and again mentioned his fear of being found out when his anus was examined. Having in mind the size of his anus after all the fucking, his fear now seemed justified. If they really did take a peep at his arsehole or even stick a finger in then everything would be clear to them. About two I gave him a lift home.

February 15th, 1992

Muslims and Serbs

Our writer in exile, Milovan Danojlić, publishes his travel stories in instalments, entitled 'A Trip to India'. Among other things, he writes about making friends with men there. "Men often hug each other on the street, tap each other on the shoulder, even hold each other's hands. Muslims do so more often than Hindus. When I told my French friend about it, she said, 'You Serbs also hug each other on the streets...' Well, maybe, but not as often as they do in Indian films" (*Borba,* February 1992).

Danojlić is right, Muslim men really like to hug and kiss each other, but even more than that. My experience, as well as that of many other homosexuals, including famous ones like Gide or Wilde, shows that Muslims really do find pleasure in male love, which does not automatically mean they are homosexual. They are probably bisexual, and go in for homosexual love because their women are often unavailable for sex. Nevertheless, even after they marry, many do not kick the habit of having occasional sex with men. This is why so many gays go on holiday to Islamic countries. I also got to know and like Muslims through sex, although once I had prejudices and an unfriendly attitude towards them, just like Jean Genet, who got to like Arabs very much.

Many of my lovers in ex-Yugoslavia were Muslims from Bosnia, Sandžak, and Albanians from Kosovo. If it wasn't for sex, which was the main reason why I met individuals of all races and nations, I probably wouldn't have such strong anti-nationalist and cosmopolitan feelings. Don Juan cannot be a nationalist because he likes all the women in the world. I am not a nationalist because I like all the young and beautiful men of the world. The sources of my cosmopolitanism and my love of all men are not to be found in my mind or in my heart, but in my cock and my arse, that is in my sex drive; it was later that my reason accepted this impulsive tendency, gave it a rational form and created an anti-nationalist attitude.

March 3rd, 1992

The Invalid in Red

I saw another invalid from the war on Prince Mihajlo Street. This time he was a nice black-haired young man of about twenty-two or three. He had no arms or legs. What was left of him was only his trunk. Another boy pushed his wheelchair. He wore a silky bright red sweatshirt and a pair of fashionable shades, raised on his forehead. He turned his head around, looking in shop windows and at passers-by. It seemed he was hungrily absorbing the life around him as if he had come from another planet. He gave me the impression of a child who was being taken out for the first time after a long illness. I had the feeling that he was a person who had been absent from this world for a long time and was now trying hard to get back into it. His face however gave no sign of awareness of the terrible tragedy that had happened to him — of the fact that he was already limbless and only twenty-three!

I suddenly felt that all the war-mongers, national leaders and mad generals should be shot — because of this young man's tragedy. They led their peoples into an outrageous civil war. And he isn't the only cripple! There are an awful lot of tortured and dead people, who died in the worst agony. It makes me sick to think that the greatest culprits of this war will probably never be tried at a court for their war crimes and never punished. Their guilt is so great that it makes every possible punishment unfitting. They would have to live a thousand times so that it would be possible to make them suffer and die in awful pain a thousand times, as so many innocent people did in this war.

My dirty mind has turned to sexual fantasies. That poor guy cannot even masturbate, not even hold his own cock in his hand. He cannot even wipe his own arse. All these things have to be done by someone else. Is that not a humiliation for a twenty-three-year-old man. He will never be able to touch another body with his hand or caress it — the body of a boy or a girl, it makes no difference. What is going on in his head, what does he think and feel? Does he still have a girlfriend, or has she left him? How do his parents feel about it all? I would like to talk with him. I like him, maybe I could even have sex with him. I'd do everything with him. It would be exciting to fuck him and to be fucked by him — the contrast between preserved sexual power and complete physical helplessness is perhaps the most exciting thing of all. Would he accept an offer to try some male love under the circumstances or is he still an unshakable heterosexual?

I think it would be both clever and humane to found some agency for sexual help to invalids which would employ volunteers of both sexes. I certainly would volunteer but unfortunately our society is too primitive to accept such an idea. Humanitarian aid involves medical care, food, wheelchairs, crutches and similar things, but it seems it hasn't occurred to anyone that these are also young people who need sex which is not available to them because of their condition. I think it would be humanitarian to help them in that field as well. As they probably do not have the money for prostitutes, volunteers would be needed.

March 9th, 1992

A False Ivan

When I went into the toilet at Staklenac I spotted a handsome blond guy with the appearance of a bully, standing in front of a urinal. Around him, there was a bunch of older men wanking with their tongues out. I stood beside him and started masturbating discreetly. He gave me a brief look and went out. I caught up with him at the entrance to the Albanija building. He gladly accepted my conversation. He told me his name was Ivan, he was twenty-one and was from Belgrade. At present he was in the army but he had several days off. He said he'd spent several days at the front in Croatia. There he was captured by members of the Croat army of so-called National Guardians (ZNG), who tortured him by beating and whipping him and putting out their cigarettes on his body. While he was talking about these things he seemed a bit lost and weird. I had the impression that he had a screw loose, which made me a little afraid, but he was too handsome for me to give up the intention of making love with him. I took him to my place.

When we arrived I offered him a drink. He had a vodka and I a cup of tea. He wasn't in the mood for talking. He was impatient to have sex, and when he thought the moment was right he jumped on me and started hugging and kissing me violently. He unzipped my trousers, took out my cock and started sucking it. All the while he was looking at me with this loony expression. He ripped all the clothes off our bodies and sat down on my cock. I gave him some cream to lubricate his arsehole and he sat all the way down. We tried different positions, I fucked him from above and lying on the side. After that he wanted to fuck me, and I accepted his wish, with the condition that he put on a condom. He fucked me lying on top of me but I wouldn't let him come inside me despite the condom. We finished off by masturbating each other. While he was showering I searched his pockets to check if he had lied to me. I saw from his documents that his name was not Ivan but Igor and that he wasn't from Belgrade but from Loznica. The only true thing was that he was in the army, as I saw his licence to be out of the barracks. I copied the data about him on a piece of paper, just in case. You never know what idea might get into the head of such a person. Caution is the mother of wisdom. Later I gave him a lift to Zeleni Venac. I gave him my phone number and he promised to call me.

April 4th, 1992

The Holy Father

Today's *Borba* contain's excerpts from the diary of the writer Živojin Pavlović, who visited the war-stricken Vukovar. Among other things, he wrote:

"When I was in the churchyard of the destroyed Orthodox church, I could almost see a black mantle over the arse of a homosexual priest, kissing bearded young chetniks whose caps were adorned with cockades as big as hands" (*Borba*, April 2nd, 1992). I think this allusion is transparent enough and that the arse in question belongs to the famous Father Filomen, a great patriot, a fighter for religious Orthodoxy and the Serb spirit. The holy father became famous through collecting humanitarian aid for soldiers at the front, by frequent participation in TV and radio programmes and by having himself photographed carrying a machine-gun in front of a Serbian tank. Despite the fact that I find Father Filomen's nationalism and war-mongering extremely repulsive I might very well rise to his defence precisely because I find the idea of him having homosexual orgies in a church quite nice.

Živojin Pavlović obviously, like me, does not like Filomen's political activities and his vulgar exaggerated patriotism. However, it is absurd to relate his political viewpoints to his sexual preferences because the result of such an attempt is again to equate enemies with homosexuals (here he is aware of homosexuality among his enemies and is blind to its existence among his political friends). I wonder if Pavlović would write similar things about a priest who falls for female charms, would he write about 'the cock of a heterosexual priest'? I do not believe he would, because a 'hot arse' is an abnormal thing whilst a 'hot cock is seen as natural. This author is also trapped by a further prejudice about homosexuals — that all homosexuals like to be fucked, not to fuck. It obviously didn't even occur to Pavlović that the holy father might be one of those who like to fuck and whose cock was hot for the tight arseholes of the young chetniks, not vice versa.

April 10th, 1992

Sexually Molested Captives

Today's *Borba* contains an article entitled 'Information by experts from the Military Academy on forms of physical and mental molestation of prisoners in Croat prisons'. Among other things, the report claims:

"Mental harassment ranged from intimidations, threats, blackmail, and various forms of humiliation, to brutal bursts of rage and homosexual and heterosexual molestations. Most frequently, harassment included:

— exposure to electric shocks with electrodes attached to genitals;

— the rape of bound women;

— the stripping and beating of prisoners with army boots and sticks until loss of consciousness;

— demanding that prisoners masturbate in front of Tito's portrait;

— forcing prisoners to masturbate in front of elderly women;

— forcing younger men to fellate elderly ones;

— anal rape of victims then forcing victims to fellate and ingest the sperm of the rapist;

— forcing captives' wives to fellate another prisoner in presence of the husband..."

I'd like to see a report by Croat doctors on forms of physical and mental molestation of captives in Serb prisons, which must be rather similar. One could make a 'comparative analysis' to find out which of the two nations is more imaginative when it comes to methods of torture and humilation.

Not long ago I heard that members of the Croat police

castrated fifty captured soldiers of the Yugoslav army. It is also said that Serbs had the custom of forcing the captured Croats to fuck and fellate each other. On one such occasion, all the Serb soldiers sat in a circle around the Croat captives, shouting abusive remarks, laughing and telling them what to do.

Of all such things, I'm of course most interested in the homosexual dimension of torture and humilation. Why does the idea of forcing soldiers of another nation to have homosexual intercourse come into the mind of a heterosexual? The main reason of course is the wish to humiliate the prisoner as much as possible and to completely destroy any human dignity. In the minds of rough macho men, the greatest possible humilation a real man can experience is his 'devirilisation' through being anally raped and various other homosexual activities. The enemy shouldn't be simply killed, he must be disgraced first, deprived of his much-respected manliness and feminised — as a man who is fucked by another becomes a sort of woman.

Another reason may lie in the torturers' suppressed homosexual desire, as they perhaps project their hidden unconscious wishes onto their captives. Since they themselves do not dare to have homosexual intercourse, as this is the greatest of taboos amongst Balkan macho males, they force prisoners to perform things they dare not do. It might be an example of latent homosexuality — this theory is old and half-rejected, but it cannot be completely false.

Finally, one of the ultimate humiliations is castration of soldiers. To cut off the penises of such young men is to humiliate them for good, to deprive them of their virility, their erotic pleasure and their offspring. A war invalid who comes back without an arm or leg becomes a hero. He can even show pride in having lost his limbs as proof of his courage and patriotism. However, a man who comes back from the war without his penis is not a man but a creature without dignity. He is ashamed of his misfortune and becomes an object of pity and occasionally even scorn. Just as a bird without wings is no longer a bird, a man without a cock is no longer a man.

I rather like the situation when heterosexuals start humiliating each other by forcing each other into homosexual intercourse. The situation has a touch of the 'theatre of the absurd'. In this situation no one is a real homosexual, neither the torturer nor the victim, and yet there is still homosexual intercourse. Heterosexuals play homosexual for the amusement of the heterosexual audience. Real homosexuals are usually absent from such situations, they are simply a remote model, a reference. It reminds me of the Japanese kabuki theatre, in which roles of both male and female characters are played by males.

July 11th, 1992

Chasing Invalids

I saw the boy without arms or legs on the island of Ada again. He was sitting on the beach leaning on his wheelchair. Two guys were sitting beside him. He was wearing only a bathing suit, so his stumps were fully visible. His friends and family were probably trying to get him back to 'normal life': taking him for a 'walk' along Prince Mihajlo Street, to the beach, to the cinema, just like before. Can anything be normal and 'like before' for this boy? Everything is reduced to tragic attempts of imitating life the way it used to be. I wonder how he, crippled like that, must have felt among the thousands of bathers with arms and legs, who ran, played ball, dived, laughed, seduced girls. How did he feel about hidden and obvious glances at his ugly stumps? What sort of normal conversation can there be between him and someone else? Can he, or can his environment, forget even for a moment that he has no legs or arms? What is his sex life look like? As a notorious sexoholic, I always think of that.

In the bushes behind the nudist beach, I met a handsome Gypsy — a hooligan I've known for some time. After a short bargaining about the price he gave me oral pleasures for two hundred dinars. It occurred to me that those two friends of the crippled guy could bring him to the bushes crowded with gays and leave him alone for a while. Since he was young and handsome, I'm sure he would attract many a good soul or at least an elderly man who would be glad to satisfy him orally. I'm certain he would like it because he most probably hadn't had sex for a long time, unless his mates brought some cheap tarts for him.

I had noticed that the Red Cross organisation frequently brings invalids and disturbed persons in wheelchairs to Ada Island for recreation. Some of them are very well-built and handsome. Having that in mind, the movement 'invalids in the bushes' could get a wide support. I can imagine the scene in which lustful invalids rush along the paths on their wheelchairs with the queens chasing after the most handsome ones. I could also imagine the degree of shock/horror of the petit-bourgeois public such scenes would lead to.

But I'm really quite serious about the idea — if young and healthy men in prison regularly have homosexual activity in the absence of women, I don't see why invalids shouldn't do the same. And since they are mostly ignorant of where to go and unable to get to such places unaided, society should help them in some way. I know some individuals are already doing that on their own initiative. I frequently see a wheelchair-bound invalid cruising at Ušće. Another, with his leg cut off, regularly cruises on his crutches at Staklenac. It appears that they have little success, but the reason may be they are middle-aged and unattractive rather than their invalidity.

August 31st, 1992

A Great and Courageous Hero

I read in today's *Politika* that Bora got killed. In the newspaper there were several notices with pictures of him in a uniform. These obituaries corresponded to the stereotype.

"Bora, you lived quietly. You had a gentle nature and a mild disposition. You died a heroic death, disappearing in the madness of the war, defending the Serb people from Croat and Muslim criminals in Bosnia, near Srebrnica, the country your ancestors fled from in 1941. You died as a proud and courageous son of the Serb people! You'll always be remembered ..."

"We inform all relatives and friends that our son and brother, a warrior in the battle of Vukovar, where he was wounded, Bora 'Wolf' died on August 25th, 1992 on the battlefield outside Srebrnica, attacking a Croat bunker and protecting the Serb people and Serb lands..."

"In great sorrow, we say our last goodbyes to our dear Bora, a great and courageous hero, who lost his life as a volunteer on the battlefield."

What is behind all this patriotic lament over the dead hero? Who was Bora really? Why did he volunteer? Did he join the war in order to defend the Serb people from Croat and Muslim 'criminals'?

I met Bora about four or five years ago. I saw him in Staklenac from time to time where he pretended he was making phone calls. He never went into the toilets. I did not dare approach him because he looked like a 'tough guy'. He had the face of a boxer, he was short but well-built, and walked with great self-consciousness, swinging his arms wide apart from his body. I found out later that he was 'one of us', despite his appearance. He mostly did sex for money but also found great pleasure in it. I had no contact with him until I met him at Milija's place one day. It was there that a number of male prostitutes gathered along with their potential customers. As he belonged to the former group and I to the latter, our interests corresponded. From then on we used to see each other from time to time and he gave me high quality sexual services at very low prices.

As I said, he did not do it simply for the money — he enjoyed having sex with men and the money was just an excuse. He sucked my cock with great skill and love every time. I often fucked him, first with no condom and then with one. He enjoyed it too although his anus was rather wide. He was able to be fucked for hours without tiring. I once organised some group sex with him. Sava and I fucked him one after the other and made him suck our cocks. I liked him because he was blond, well-built and practically hairless. However, Bora did not choose his customers, he did it with anyone who offered him enough money and did everything his clients wanted. In contrast to his 'secret' life he also had an open public life where he dated girls and went out with his heterosexual friends. From the point of view of society and family-centred morals he had a 'normal' way of life. He was quiet and unobstrusive by nature, he did not talk much and had nothing much to say even when he did talk. The newspaper obituary was therefore quite right to mention that he lived quietly and had a gentle nature and mild disposition. He'd had no schooling to talk of so he had to work at odd jobs for the Youth Cooperative or workshop owners, but I never heard he went in for illegal activities.

Let me get back to my previous question: why did he volunteer? I don't think the reason was fanatic patriotism at all. In his everyday life he was a 'nobody' — he had no job, nor was he involved in any other activity or social task which would have increased his self-esteem and social kudos. The war gave him the opportunity to be a 'somebody'. The uniform he wore as a volunteer gave him a role and a highly esteemed place in society. He became a 'Serb fighter', a potential hero. Showing off all around Belgrade in camouflage clothing was very appealing for young men like him. If they carried a weapon then they put on even more airs. They enjoyed talking about their war adventures and exploits. Such stories usually centred on how they escaped certain death or on how many Croat and Muslim soldiers they had killed. Getting wounded in battle also contributed to one's reputation. Before he was killed Bora was wounded once in the battle around Vukovar so he already had the aura of a hero. His second most important reason was being bored. I think he was hopelessly bored with his life and the war offered the opportunity of running away from monotonous everyday life and having some fun. This is no new phenomenon, there are authors who have discovered that for some people war is a sort of 'tourist vacation'. One of his reasons might also have been his wish to get rich.

There were rumours in Belgrade that a lot of fighters and 'heroes' returned from the war with very expensive war trophies. Members of various paramilitary formations and volunteer squads got especially rich. They not only robbed Croat and Muslim homes but also those of Serbs. They often took everything they could lay their hands on — money, gold, jewellery, cars, TV sets, videos, etc. I read somewhere that many even took washbasins, bath tubs, toilets and tiles. All these things were loaded on trucks carted away and sold. Members of these military units used to say that anybody who had not made at least a hundred thousand deutschmark must have been an utter idiot. I do not want to say bad things about a dead person but I think this kind of thinking was not unfamiliar to Bora.

Finally there is a category of pathological maniacs who go to war to satisfy their darkest murderous and sexual drives. They find great satisfaction in war through being able to torture their captives cruelly, to humiliate them, forcing them to submit, destroying the last remnants of human dignity, raping their victims be they men, women, boys or girls. Things we already know about brutal crimes happening on all sides are horrifying and I expect we'll find out even worse when the war is finally over.

As for Bora I cannot say he had such base impulses. A lot of young men from poor working-class and peasant families and even petit-bourgeois families joined the war for one or more of the aforementioned reasons. For them 'the fight for Serb homes and territories' was just a good excuse and a disguise for their real reasons. Therefore it is hardly surprising that many famous criminals and mafia members became great patriots and Serbophiles almost overnight. They were the first to join the war, stealing everything they could and becoming wealthy, returning home as war heroes and respectable citizens. These gangsters became the models for numerous boys who followed in their footsteps hoping to get rich. Many of them lost their lives because of their greed.

I know personally many such young men from the bottom, who used to prostitute themselves to men and volunteered in the war hoping to achieve some of those goals. Beli also took part in the war, he got wounded in the leg and didn't manage to steal anything. Goran, a large boxer, a thief and a cheat, was even promoted and held rank in the regular army. I saw him a couple of months ago strutting around. He was especially proud of his 'TT' gun, hung on his waist. Tall blond Dejan, who spent some time in jail for cheating and stealing, has been in Bosnia for more than a year now. I heard he'd got himself killed — if true that would be a great pity as he had the biggest cock I had ever seen.

November 2nd, 1992

Between Hammer and Anvil

I spent the whole afternoon cruising unsuccessfully. In the evening I went to Karadjordje Park. I spent some time talking with some familiar guys and made a couple of rounds. I saw three suspicious-looking men enter the park from the Oncology Clinic entrance. They walked along the whole path once then sat down on a bench. I managed to get out of the park inconspicuously onto the Yugoslav National Army Boulevard. I was standing at the tram stop across the street and watching what was going on. From the bigger park they went into the smaller one and I was able to see their faces under the light. They looked rough and crude, sweaty, dirty and unshaven, rather like seasonal labourers from Bosnia. When they entered the smaller park I first heard a short row, then screams and cries for help: "Ouch! Help! Thieves! Police! Ouch!"

They were beating up a homosexual and there was no one there to help him. Those who heard his screams, like me, did not dare come to his aid for fear that they might be beaten up themselves. I stood still listening to his screams. I just did not know what to do — how could I help him? If I had been strong enough or familiar with martial arts I would have strangled those criminals with my bare hands. In this case I simply had to listen to his cries — what could I do, I felt so helpless! Suddenly after quick thinking I jumped into my car, turned on the lights and rushed onto the main footpath. When they saw my car drive into the park with full headlights on the attackers ran away towards Slavija Circus. The guy who'd been their victim also ran off, obviously thinking I was the police.

I just saw his silhouette, I couldn't see how wounded he was, but he was probably okay since he could run. I drove on to Slavija to see where the hoodlums were going. They went as far as MacDonald's, walking calmly and about to go in. They were probably going to treat themselves with the money they'd stolen from their victim. I was desperate because I could do nothing to have them arrested and punished.

★★★

A couple of years ago I was attacked in Yugodrag Park, next to the Yugoslav Drama Theatre. I was cruising along the path parallel with Marshal Tito Street which wasn't dark at all because it was illuminated by the bright street lights. I felt safe because of that. I was approached by two decently dressed guys and asked the time. They looked a bit suspicious, but I still didn't expect them to attack me so near a busy street. I was wrong! As soon as I cast a glance at my watch they started hitting me. They hit me with their hands and fists on the head then knocked me down on the ground. Then they started to put the boot in and calling me names. I shouted, "Help! Help! Police!" but no-one heard me or if they did pretended not to hear. Nobody came to my aid — they went on hitting and kicking me for as long as they wished. When they left I could hardly get to my feet and limp to the car. I looked at my face in the rear-view mirror — it was bloody and swollen and my nose was broken. I touched it and it moved making cracking sounds.

I was horrified. I drove fast to the nearest hospital. They didn't want to see me there because all the doctors were off duty. They sent me to the Surgical Clinic where I had problems because I didn't have my health insurance papers. Nevertheless they finally let me in for treatment. My head was X-rayed and my face washed. They concluded that my nose bone was broken and I had haematomas under my eyes. They gave me a local anaesthetic and then arranged my nose with a metal instrument resembling those used by butchers. They put plaster over my nose and fastened it down with sticking-plaster. With that awful thing on my nose, swollen face and black and blue circles under my eyes I must have looked a right freak , a bit like the 'elephant man'. The worst moment was when my parents saw me. I made up some story about being mugged on the street. It took more than a month for everything to heal up. When they actually removed the nasal dressing it turned out that they hadn't fixed the nose properly, it was all crooked. I later had to go to Switzerland for a proper nose-job.

That evening when leaving the Surgical Clinic I looked at my wrist and noticed my watch was gone. My wrist was scratched. The attackers had probably forced the watch off my wrist and since it had a metal strap my wrist was covered with bruises. It was an expensive Tissot watch I had bought in Geneva. Before I go back to the story about that watch I must talk about the history of my watches. The first watch I ever had, a 'Marvin', was given to me by my father. It was his old watch and he gave it to me when he bought himself a new one. I used it for a couple of years and when I started to lead a double life and cruising around parks, it was taken from me. A guy whom I had sex with in Kalemegdan took it from me. I told Dad I'd lost it because the strap was loose. He was angry. He said I was irresponsible and that I didn't deserve to get another watch. Nevertheless, he bought me a Tissot watch for my birthday when we were living in Geneva. I used it for a year and it was again taken from me. I met a tall blond guy in the toilet on Quai des Bergues in Geneva. He was standing there in front of a urinal, wanking and smiling at me. I liked him. We went out and introduced ourselves. He told me his name was Albert and that he was French from Lyon. I couldn't take him to my place, since I lived with my parents, so I took him to the room of a friend of mine who had given me the keys. The room by the way, was at the Catholic Youth Hostel — run by nuns.

When we got there I played the record of the famous gay song by Charles Aznavour, *Comme ils disent*. I started kissing his neck and mouth while the song was playing. At the time the song was a hit in all of Geneva's gay bars. I touched his zip fastener but his cock was still soft. Aznavour was singing: "J'habite seul avec maman, dans un très vieil appartement... pour me faire compagnie j'ai deux chattes et un canari... souvent je fais le marché et la cuisine... je pique aussi à la machine, mais mon vrai métier c'est la nuit ou j'exerce le travesti... oui, je suis un homo, comme ils disent." At that moment he asked me where the bathroom was — I opened the door and showed him the way. At this modest hotel none of the rooms had en suite bathrooms but there was a communal one on each floor. He was gone for quite a while and when he came back into the room Aznavour was finishing his song "l'objet de tous mes tourments passe le plus clair de son temps au lit des femmes... oui, je suis un homo..." I approached him and put my arms around his shoulders.

At that very moment I felt something cold and hard against my neck. I was terrified when I saw it was a knife and with hatred in his eyes and a threatening voice he asked me to hand over all my money. Without speaking I gave him fifty Swiss francs which was all I had on me at the time. He wasn't satisfied and started searching my pockets; he took my diplomatic papers and the Tissot watch given me by my father. He was pressing his knife into me all the time we were out on the street. Before he disappeared he said that if I bought him three hundred francs that evening at nine o'clock he'd give me my watch back. He said he'd wait at the railway station entrance.

I was desperate — how could I face my father without that watch he'd given me and the missing diplomatic papers? I gathered all my courage and went to the police station hoping they would help me find the criminal. I started retelling the story of what had happened but as soon they realised it had something to do with homosexuality one of the cops said scornfully: "Ah, encore une histoire des pédés!" When I heard this I got furious, stood up and went out. Before I went out I said ironically: "Merci beaucoup de votre aide!" I managed to find the three hundred francs and went at the appointed time to the railway station entrance. The gangster, needless to say, did not appear. He was probably afraid that I'd set a police trap for him. I got home late that evening, my parents were sleeping and next morning I went quickly to a department store and bought myself a Tissot identical to the one I'd had. Dad never found out anything about the robbery, he thought the watch I wore on my wrist was the one he'd given me. The watch I'd bought was then taken from me during the attack in Belgrade I described above. Since then I've given up buying expensive watches; I go for Swatch or Casio and don't mind if they get stolen.

★★★

There's no homosexual anywhere in the world who hasn't been the victim of violence at least once in their lives. Homosexuals are always — at least in my country — between hammer and anvil. On the one hand they are victims of various criminals, thieves and teenage delinquents, who attack them just for the fun of it or for money; on the other they are often victims of the police, who instead of defending them, often perform violence on them, ranging from verbal abuse to physical punishment. Violence is done in those places where gays, forced by bad circumstances, have to gather, like public toilets, parks, even some restaurants and discothèques.

Staklenac is top of the danger list. All the shop assistants know that homosexuals cruise there. Most of them treat us with hatred and scorn. Staklenac has never been a safe place and there have always been attacks. It happens that hoodlums go in to take a leak and see that all the urinals are occupied by homosexuals jerking off. Then they use their fists, sticks and bars to make the gays go. The police come occasionally, not to catch the attackers but to beat and pursue the homosexuals. Once, they locked some people in the toilet and then cruelly beat them with clubs. At such moments cleaning ladies feel triumphant.

Even so, since the economic blockade of Yugoslavia and the enormous inflation, the situation in Staklenac has deteriorated. Why? There is a connection between the blockade, inflation and gays. The enormous inflation is the reason why there is such a large black market of foreign money traders, dealers mostly recruited from the mass of Bosnian refugees who rolled down from their wild mountains to the centre of Belgrade. Money dealers are mostly concentrated on Prince Mihajlo Street, especially in front of the Albanija building, around one of the entrances to Staklenac. They stand there shouting "Money! Money!" During their 'working hours' they go to the toilet several times and find the urinals always occupied with people just standing there. At the beginning it probably seemed strange to these people but when they realised that the men standing around were in fact wanking, they understood they were gays and this made them furious.

Their 'healthy sense of morality' couldn't cope with such scandalous behaviour in the centre of Belgrade. They started a systematic war against gays, going into the toilets several times a day and beating with their fists and wooden sticks everyone they found there. Even non-homosexual men were beaten up. They hit one boy's head so hard against the wall that he was covered in blood. Even an elderly man got beaten up. When he found some police officers and complained to them they replied, "Beat it or we'll beat you!" In contrast the police are very friendly with illegal dealers, often stopping to chat with them, whispering confidences, money changing hands from dealer to police. They collaborate with the very people they are supposed to pursue and arrest. Another reason for the friendly relations between the new Bosnian inhabitants and the police is that large numbers of the police are Bosnian too. Some of them knew each other before coming to Belgrade. I don't want to sound like the conceited son of 'an old Belgrade family', the kind of person who hates all newcomers to Belgrade, looking down particularly on Bosnians. I don't care where someone comes from or what a person's nationality might be, but I hate crude, primitive people and most of the refugees I happen to meet are like that. It is true however that I have met many very nice, clever and witty Bosnians in gay circles so I do not want to generalise my observations. But since the attacks of those Bosnians began, Staklenac has become a very dangerous place at any time of the day.

It happened once that I was exchanging glances with a tall handsome guy carrying an Adidas bag over his shoulder, in front of the telephone booth there. He walked on slowly, looking back at me, and I started following him. He stopped in front of each shop window and looked back at me. This technique is typical of street cruising. I hesitated about approaching him because he seemed a bit like a hoodlum. I finally did, however, and asked him the time. He asked me angrily, not with a Bosnian accent like I expected but with a Montenegrian one, "Why are you following me, huh!"

I was somewhat taken aback by the question because I thought it was clear. I was confused, so I mumbled something. He suddenly took a big gun from his jacket and said, "Maybe that idiot Durović sent you to follow me?" "No! no! who's Durović? I've no idea!" I murmured, paralysed with fear, looking with my eyes wide open at the gun pointed at me. "Don't lie! Come on, beat it before I make a hole in you!" I turned around dizzy from the shock and ran up the stairs to the Albanija building. Incredible! In the very centre of town, in a busy underground passage, a guy threatens to shoot me with a gun. He wasn't afraid or ashamed before all the people who were passing by. Later I realised that he had no idea why I was following him or that I was gay. He was probably a criminal from Montenegro, just passing through Belgrade or 'working' here temporarily, and he thought I was tailing him as a member of another gang, or something like that. I could have been shot.

After all these events I cut down on my visits to Staklenac, and when I did go there I was extremely careful. I was afraid I might meet that guy again while he was using the phone there — then he would be sure I was following him and shoot me.

★★★

The other dangerous places are the park at Ušće and Karadjordje Park — or as we call it 'Kara-djoka' (cock-prick) or 'Hydropark' (because a meteorological station is situated there). Homosexuals who go there are often attacked by teenage gangs. They go there in groups of five to ten people, sometimes more. They are more and more often armed with heavy metal chains, screwdrivers and similar weapons. When they don't have such tools they use their fists and feet to beat their victims. Their attacks are usually sudden and quick. They rush into the park and the bushes, beating up and robbing everyone they meet there. They take money, watches, gold chains, as well as nice jackets, Nike or Reebok trainers and so on. Even when they don't want to steal they beat people just for fun. They pass by the park, discussing aloud whether they should go in and beat up people or not. Sometimes they are in the mood for such entertainment, other times not — it's a kind of sport with them, a bit like martial arts training. When they have nothing much to do and are bored they'll turn to beating up homosexuals. There are even children from rich families in such groups, who don't need to take anything from anybody. I have the impression that they don't think they're doing wrong, immoral or cruel. On the contrary, it is a positive and acceptable thing to beat faggots. Everybody hates fags, so they should be eliminated when they get too numerous. Just like hunters organise wolf or fox hunts because those animals supposedly attack poultry and livestock, so it is completely acceptable to organise gay-hunts from time to time.

After all, isn't the law against us? One year in prison for men caught having sex together. The public ignore attacks on gays, and the police have more important business to attend to than to prosecute the attackers. The police react only if someone has been killed. The investigation in such cases consists of calling and taking into custody all homosexuals they have on their files for interrogation — although it is clear in 99 per cent of such cases that fellow homosexuals were not the murderers. The police say they do this because they need to get information on possible murderers. I don't know if they do it because they are amused to see so many homosexuals beaten in interrogation rooms or whether they just like to create an illusion for themselves and their bosses that they are busy doing something useful and thus earning their salary.

It happens sometimes that various sorts of maniacs or mentally disturbed persons go to the dark parks. They always go alone. Usually they'll attack from the bushes — sometimes threatening people with guns and forcing ones they fancy to fellate them. It happened to a good friend of mine and I don't doubt his story. There have been even more dangerous situations. A couple of years ago, a maniac cut the throat of a medical student because he wouldn't do what he ordered. He cut his artery, blood spurted out, the maniac ran away and the student fell and died before the ambulance arrived. I read soon after that the police had succeeded in capturing the murderer. After all the attacks and dangers gay activities have almost completely stopped at Ušće. Only a few enthusiasts go there now and only during the day, but even that isn't safe. A gang of

Gypsies robbed a guy in the bushes in broad daylight recently. They even took his clothes. Fortunately a friend of the victim, who'd also been cruising, was able to go home and bring some clothes back for the poor guy. Only the bravest or craziest ones enter Karadjordje Park. Not only teenage gangs roam the place but also the police frequently raid using their batons. Therefore most people don't cruise there but now cruise by the tram stop across the street, in front of St Sava Temple or at the station in front of the Medical Centre. Some people go cruising and make love in the dark bushes between the hospital buildings on Jovan Subotić Street. But it isn't safe there either since the police found out what was going on. Homosexuals are like pursued animals — always running before their hunters.

★★★

A third group of dangerous places are the toilets at the bus and railway stations. In our local gay parlance the former is known as Busette and the latter as Railette. These places are actually not that dangerous unless the people who go there are too intrusive and stupid. It sometimes happens that some too courageous gay stares at the cock of someone who just comes in to take a leak so obviously and conspicuously that the man reacts violently, shouting "You mother-fucking faggot!" and beating him. The same happens when someone peeps under the door of a booth or climbs on a radiator to see what the occupants are doing. There are even those who try to get into occupied booths by force, in many such cases it happens that a raging person emerges from the booth and starts beating people up — the real culprit having already fled. There are some guys who entice elderly gay guys to a booth, by jerking off with the door open. When the victim enters the booth he will be robbed whilst being fucked or be seriously threatened with a knife. It is also dangerous to make love in the booth as they are regularly raided by the police. They just rush into the toilet and kick open the booth doors, looking for those with two men inside. Sometimes they are more cunning and then they too peep under the doors to see who is inside and what is going on. Sometimes the cleaners call the police when they see two men going into the same booth. I was there once when something like this was going on. A cleaning lady was showing a cop a booth where she'd noticed two gay guys enter. The cop bent down and peeped under the door. When he saw two pairs of legs, he exchanged a triumphant smile with the denouncer. They waited for the two guys to come out of the booth and then caught them. I couldn't linger any longer in the toilet without looking suspicious. So I didn't see what happened. When cops catch two guys together in a booth or even when they see somebody standing in front of a urinal masturbating, they beat them there or take them to a small room next to the left luggage office called among gays 'the intensive care'. There they are harassed, humiliated, kicked and beaten with batons.

I know of a middle-aged man whom they'd caught standing in front of a urinal. First they beat him up cruelly in the toilet, then hit him with their batons, then knocked him down kicking him and shouting insults all the time. One cop even put a gun to his head and finally handcuffed him and threw him out. He was taken to the 'intensive care' where he was handcuffed to a radiator and his beating continued. I even heard of a guy who was caught by one policeman who took him to the 'intensive care' and forced him to give him a blow job. He also forced him to swallow all the sperm so that no drops were left on the floor. I don't really believe this story because it sounds like a product of the popular homoerotic fantasy in which place, uniform and force play key roles. But although it sounds pretty unlikely, such a case is not impossible.

The police also have the habit of rushing into toilets and interrogating everybody they find there whether gay or straight. As the toilet is constantly busy with large numbers of real passengers who have no idea of what's going on the police have real difficulties trying to find out who is gay and who isn't. Of course no one admits to anything. Therefore the police have invented a method probably copied from films. One of them sits together with the cleaning lady in her glass booth, they then turn off the lights in her booth and another cop starts taking toilet users one by one to the booth. The point of the whole exercise is for the cleaning lady to identify the gays — she knows which persons use the facility every day. Those who aren't recognised as gays by the cleaner are released. The gays are taken for an interrogation, beaten up or taken to the 'intensive care'. The destiny of many people in there depends on the memory and mercy of the cleaners.

★★★

I am fed up with the humiliation and violence from delinquents on the one hand and the police on the other. We are always between the hammer and the anvil. We can't do anything against the violence done to us by the police as long as non-democratic conservative regimes are in power backed up by a primitive public opinion burdened with patriarchal prejudices and subject to manipulation through the media. Nevertheless something can be done against teenage gangs and hoodlums. We should just be well organised and create gay gangs. Among homosexuals there are many people who work out, are in the army or the police and are good at street fighting. They could form a gang of perhaps ten to fifteen people who would have a mission of defence and revenge. Some of these young gangsters should be caught, made to suck everyone's dick and swallow sperm and then have their headst fucked off. They should be completely humiliated and unmanned.

Fucked-out like that, let them go and complain to their mums and dads. After that I'd stick a candle up their arse and let them go home like that. Those who are again caught beating gays should be castrated. I get so angry! That would be such a small revenge for what they did to Dragan who remained paralysed after they'd beaten him up, for Srdjan whose head was broken, for me who had a nasal bone fracture, and for many other beaten, humiliated or murdered homosexuals. Revenge is necessary; accounts should be settled for once.

Sometimes I dream of my own revenge, like 'Zorro the Avenger'. If I ever come to catch a fatal disease, I intend to apply my vengeful scenario. I would buy a big knife, like in the film *Psycho*, wait in the bushes for one of the rowdies and stick the knife in his neck. Unfortunately I would manage to kill only one of them that way, maybe a gang would manage to disarm me, so I wouldn't do anything. A better thing for me would be to buy a machine-gun, like a Kalashnikoff or Uzi (they are easy to buy from soldiers and mafiosi on the black market), go to the park and hide in the bushes and wait patiently for hoodlums to appear. When they entered the park I would jump out of the bushes and shout, with my gun concealed, "Hey guys! Have you come to beat fags?" They would probably answer, "Yes, where are they?" Then I would reply, "Here, I'm one. Come and get me!" At that moment when they start toward me I would take out my machine-gun and shoot in their direction. They would fall down and cry. The ones I missed would flee in panic, shouting "Run! Run! The madman's shooting!"

I would approach those lying on the ground and finish them off. Then I would put the gun in my own mouth and pull the trigger. That's where my vengeful dream ends.

November 21st, 1992

A Duke or a Duchess?

The last number of the *Duga* weekly contains one of the fiercest and most direct criticisms of 'Duke' Šešelj (the leader of the Radical Party, the most powerful right-wing party in Serbia) concerning his supposed homosexuality. Branko Lainović, the ex-commander of the so-called Serb Elite Guard, uses the feminine gender when he is referring to Šešelj, to express his disgust and disdain towards him and his political activities: "That hairless heap of flesh and fat did not have the guts to do anything else, but to start rumours about the late Giska... She also told lies about me. I don't hold it against her, because every woman I did not want to make love with has the right to be angry. Mrs Vojka Šešelj would be better advised to take up housework and leave the men's work to us men or to participate in elections, together with the communists in San Francisco, the famous gay capital. It is only there that she has a good chance of winning under fair conditions."

This is only one of many assaults and insinuations concerning Šešelj's suspicious masculinity. In September 1991, Djindjić, a deputy of the Democratic Party, wondered "How can a chetnik duke be beardless?" and concluded that he is maybe a chetnik duchess. Šešelj replied that his beard is so strong that he has to shave twice a day. After that quip a magazine published a photograph of him standing in front of a mirror, his face covered with cream, shaving his strong masculine beard. In his reply to Djindjić, Šešelj made a counter-attack, saying that his voice was deeper than his opponent's, which was a strong proof that his masculinity was superior. He also maintained that Djindjić had once worn an earring, bringing his masculinity into question.

So, while the country was on the verge of civil war, and the economic and social crisis was getting increasingly serious, our representatives were trying to measure the length of each other's beards and the depth of their voices in order to prove which of them was the toughest man! *O tempora, o mores!*

Students aren't very fond of Šešelj either, which is obvious from the following newspaper report published in *Borba* (July 10th, 1992), dealing with student demonstrations. "Šešelj tried to stop the demonstrations, threatening people with a gun. Their fear turned into fury, because the students realised that Šešelj's presence was a planned provocation. They started chanting 'Faggot, faggot!', and a large group of students rushed towards the duke. In the statement he made to *Borba* (Aug 4th, 1992) on the foundation of the Agency for Political Marketing, the famous journalist Zoran Petrović-Piroćanac said: "We will work for all those who support the democratic option. But our agency is closed for such parties like the party of the Serb Ernest Röhm. It is an anti-democratic, fascist and essentially anti-Serb party, and we would not work for them even if they paid with gold."The columnist Tirnanić also refers to Šešelj as to a domestic version of Röhm, in the *Borba* of September 12th, 1992:"We have our own, domestic replicas of Horst Wessel, Ernst Röhm and Dr Mengele. Wessel was a prostitute (a gigolo), Röhm was a homosexual, and Dr Mengele's name became a common noun in the Serb language."

What is there behind all these insinuations and attacks on Šešelj. There have been rumours in Belgrade for a long time now that Šešelj had numerous homosexual adventures during the time he spent in prison, under the old communist regime. According to some sources he got a liking for it and started practising homosexual activities, whereas another story says that he was raped there by Muslims, and now he is trying to get revenge on them by killing whenever he gets the opportunity — his paramilitary units play an active role in battles and ethnic cleansing in Bosnia. Once the rumours started they could not be stopped. His political opponents use them from time to time to discredit him. He defended himself, not only by accusations directed at others and having himself photographed while shaving, but he also married a pretty young woman immediately, in order to destroy the suspicion. He also attacked the so-called 'democratic opposition' in a TV interview once for being so base and perverted as to accuse him of being a homosexual without any proof. Incidentally he brought up this question himself without prompting from the interviewer. It appears that he had discovered what people were saying about him and wanted to protect himself somehow. His defences were probably successful because his opponents' accusations have had no negative impact on his political career.

The reasons for this should be looked for in the naivety and prejudices of our traditionalists towards homosexuals. Most people imagine homosexuals as effeminate types with squeaky voices who use make-up and sometimes wear women's clothes. They think a homosexual is easily recognised with the help of this popular cliché. As Šešelj is a large man and speaks with a deep voice, shaves twice a day and has no effeminate gestures, he couldn't possibly — according to them — be homosexual. They have no idea that there are masculine homosexuals who cannot be recognised by voice, beard or size. So, for them, Šešelj is not a homosexual and that's that. It is a general rule that it is unmportant whether something is true or false, what is important is that it looks true and that people believe it to be true. People are often more prone to believe a falsehood than the truth. As for politicians, it is not important whether you are homosexual or not as long as it looks that you are not.

February 4th, 1993

The Rape of Your Own Grandmother

Dragoš Kalajić, our dandyish rightist intellectual, an unrecognised painter and an arrogant snob, attacks homosexuals from time to time. In the speech he made before a group of like-minded people at the launch party organised by Isidora Bjelica for her book *Notorious*, he said:

"You can say that you are a homosexual, a drug addict, or that you would like to rape your own grandmother, that would not upset anyone, but saying you are a rightist is the last taboo in this world" (*Borba*, February 4th,1993). Kalajić is wrong, either consciously or not. As opposed to what he said, being a rightist and a nationalist is very popular in Serbia nowadays, while on the other hand being a homosexual is quite difficult and scandalous (drug addicts and nationalist fighters who rape not only elderly women but also small girls, usually receive better treatment than homosexuals). Kalajić's homophobic obsession can be analysed in several ways. According to one of them the fiercest enemies of homosexuals are actually latent homosexuals who project their self-contempt onto others. Another is to see him as a homosexual who is trying to conceal his real identity by accusing others of what he is himself. There have been many such cases throughout history. I simply can't say to which group Mr Kalajić belongs, but his spruced-up image, his dandyism and his intellectual snobbishness have always looked a bit suspicious and unmanly for a 'tough guy' from the Balkans.

Kalajić has been involved in the anti-homosexual crusade for a long time. I remember one of his texts published in *Duga* ten years or more ago, where he wrote ironically about Pasolini. According to him, Pasolini used to come to recording sessions directly from his nighttime adventures, with his arse covered in blood, at the time when he was filming in Africa. I wonder if Kalajić was there and saw in person Pasolini's arse, or if the information was given to him by one of his fascist informers. In his completely unnoticed, pseudo-philosophical and quasi-visionary book *The End of the World* (Zagreb, 1979), Kalajić sees things unseen by others, numerous signs which indicate the end of the Western world. One of these signs undoubtedly is the spread of homosexuality: "With the collapse of morality, homosexualism has become a massive pastime, so, by increasing in quantity, it has lost some qualitative contents it previously had... The present structures of Western society and culture show a breakdown of masculine and moral energies and forces, a breakdown which has given way to low morale and a general feeling of tolerance... Homosexuality today is trying to conquer the planet and establish a totalitarian 'gay rule'... Utopian projects of a new society are being made in the top superstructures of the homosexual world today."

Shrewd Kalajić accepts completely the idea of the interrelation between homosexuality and the collapse of the Euro-American culture, although he sees homosexuality not as a cause but as a result of the decadence and degeneration of the West. He obviously misuses the once-popular Spenglerian theory of the decline of the West, which was earlier frequently misused by communist regimes. However, they collapsed whilst waiting for the West to do so. The Western world by contrast is developing uninterruptedly, despite the fact that it is quite tolerant towards homosexuals, giving them rights which were quite inconceivable in most communist and other totalitarian regimes. 'The decaying West' is one of the key phrases of Bolshevism, a phrase taken from Russian populists and Slavophiles in the first half of the nineteenth century, which is now going through a revival due to the rise of the nationalist movement in Russia. They fight against Westerners and the impact of West European civilisation, creating theories about an original, special and unique direction of Russia's historic development. Ideologists employed by Yugoslav rulers also claim that Serbia has a special unique direction, and a special 'mission' in this world. The worn-out thesis about the 'sick West' and the 'healthy East' is being made again by nationalists, regardless of the fact that the former is in progress and the latter in chaos. This time salvation for the East is not in the form of communism any more but in the form of Orthodoxy and a resurrected Pan-Slavism.

One of the reasons given as a cause of Western degeneracy is that Western culture became alienated from the masculine ideal, either in the form of the heroic battle for freedom of the Dinaric highlanders or in the form of fighting for social justice waged, according to communist theories, by proletarians. Therefore homosexuality as a radical negation of epic masculinity, however apolitical it may be seen under normal circumstances, now becomes a medium of a kind of propaganda. The policy of the ruling structures is not based on rational political categories but on myths and heroic epics. Being a homosexual means being an 'unmanly' man, which is, in the eyes of a traditional Balkan male, the greatest offence and a negation of the essence of his existence. Therefore, 'faggot' is one of his greatest insults. Being a homosexual or being brought into any sort of connection with homosexuality is very dangerous and disgraceful. Patriarchal heroes want only to be warriors, as it is the 'toughest' profession, whereas any other job is for women and parasites.

Back to Kalajić. In one of his numerous articles in *Duga* (July 8th, 1989), he displayed 'a great concern' over the fate of Croatia affected by the expansion of homosexuality in the country: "Enemies of Croatia are, among other things, using the propaganda of homosexuality as an effective method of subversion, aimed at demolishing European and Christian morality as the base of the Croatian spirit. Mass media in Zagreb are a proof of this as they are a means of spreading and strengthening the tendency to create homosexual apologetics." According to a recent statement made by Dr Smiljković, one of the leaders of the ruling party, it seems that enemies of Serbia similarly use the apologetics of homosexuality in their efforts to destroy Serb, Orthodox and Slavic morality. All this reminds me of mutual accusations between Nazi Germany and Communist Russia about homosexuality flourishing on the other side.

Last, in his constant search for enemies of Serbia, its morale and patriarchal values, Kalajić labelled the staff of the Students' Radio Station B-92 (which at the time organised the campaign entitled 'Fighting for Peace') as "a group of American mercenaries and national defeatists who propagandise homosexuality" (*Borba*, November 1st, 1991).

The present wave of this homophobic hysteria was joined by the leader of the Serb National Renewal Party, a minor right-wing party, whose main ideologist is none other than Mr Kalajić. At a meeting, Jović protested against "the occupation and siege of Europe carried out by Indo-Arabic and black hordes, which bring nothing but drugs and homosexuality to us" (*Politika*, October 7th, 1991). In this case, the decadent West is not the side accused of endangering our 'healthy nation' in its moral sense. In keeping with the old rightist cliché which involves overt racism, 'impure races' such as Indian, Arabic and Afro-Caribbean are accused of menacing Europe with homosexuality and drugs. 'Poor, innocent' white Europeans probably would not know what drugs and homosexuality were if it wasn't for the perverse coloured intruders. Kalajić should have told the leader of his party that homosexuality is a universal phenomenon which is not limited by time or space, present in all nations at similar extents. He could have reminded him that the greatest flourishing and confirmation of homosexual love took place in Europe, in Ancient Greece.

February 7th, 1993

Old Milija

I went to Milija's place today, for his eightieth birthday party. No one would guess he is that old, not only because of his looks, but also because of his behaviour and way of living. He is very lively, he walks fast and has energetic movements, without anything effeminate in him. His hair looks like a brush — this was always his nickname — he dyes it black regularly, and he has a thin moustache giving him the air of a fatal seducer. Once he asked me to bring him back some hair and moustache colour from Paris.

He often has sex with young lads and the funny point in it all is that it is he who fucks them. He says that his crane is still able to lift! Or that the thing is still of 'a perpendicular nature'. Of course he pays for such sexual services, since gerontophiles attracted to an eighty-year-old man are still hard to find. He keeps a meticulous record of his sexual adventures. He has cards with names of his lovers, amounts paid to them, and if he managed to fuck someone the card has a small circle on it. He likes to brag of the number of such small circles he marked during a month. When he comes across a big, thick cock, he can't resist sitting down on it. I had several opportunities to watch him making love, he usually bends over a couch and shouts: "Shove it in — like a nail into a wooden fence!" I cannot help laughing when he mention 'nails and fences'.

Milija's spirit is obviously younger than his body. He keeps talking all the time, he is interested in politics, he is an active member of the Serb Radical Party, attends demonstrations, goes out to cafés and takes trips.

I met Milija more than ten years ago. I was taken to his place by Darko, a friend of mine from Split. He'd heard from an acquaintance that this old man's flat in Belgrade was a meeting place for handsome guys who do it for money. Though I was living in Belgrade at the time I had heard nothing about it at all. When Darko came to visit me I was quite suspicious, so he had to convince me to go there. I didn't believe we'd find anything interesting. I was wrong! I was impressed by the number of handsome, manly young men who frequented Milija's apartment. The strange thing was that I didn't know any of them from the gay circles I moved in. They didn't go cruising in public places but came to Milija's instead for money, fun and drink.

Each day between six and nine o'clock his eighteen-square-metre apartment was host to two categories of people — elderly or middle-aged gentlemen, Milija's friends, and youngsters between sixteen and twenty-five. The former were clients, the latter 'merchandise'. It wasn't a classic brothel as Milija didn't take any money or provision for his services. It was more of a fresh flesh market where clients took a youngster or two they had met before. It was a very useful exchange, clients exchanged the young men and the latter exchanged clients. Of course there were 'unexpected developments', when two handsome men had sex with each other. Such combinations made Milija furious, he labelled such guys 'faggots', 'whores', 'sissies', etc. This kind of thing disturbed the system he established, as well as the illusion that the young men who came to his place were not gay but 'real men', who did it with other men only for money. Prices of sexual services from these youngsters varied from one case to another, depending on the 'quality of what was offered', and the wishes and financial abilities of clients. Of course, inflation influenced the price variations, but the average price during last ten years or so has been between ten and twenty deutschmark. During the period of the high inflation, the price was as low as two marks. There were cases however when Milija paid as much as fifty deutschmark to some of his favourites.

From the moment I came to Milija's place for the first time I used to go there at least twice or three times a week. I became a regular client. I cannot remember the number of youngsters I met there. I used to take some of them home but most of the time we'd have sex there. Occasionally Milija would go out of the room in which I made love with someone, which was his only room, so he was forced to sit in the bathroom, but he usually stayed in the room lying down and taking a nap. I didn't mind I felt no shame before him. As I said, everybody brought young guys. Older clients brought in guys they'd just met on their cruising rounds and gave them to others in order to give their pick-ups the opportunity to earn more. Moreover youngsters would bring their friends, even their brothers. They all found a mutual interest in that unusual exchange of sex and money.

I took a lot of guys there, mostly those I picked up at the railway station. The guys I took to Milija's were those I was too afraid to take back to my own flat because they looked a bit rough. In time a friendship developed with the young men. They started attending his dinner parties or just dropped in for coffee or a drink. Milija does them various favours, but they help him too. They go shopping for him, tidy his flat, give him haircuts, clip his nails, change his light bulbs and fuses and so on. Some of the guys got married and had children yet they still drop by, sometimes even with their children. Milija buys them chocolate. Some of the men graduated from university, became businessmen or gangsters and got rich, but they still find time to visit the elderly pimp.

His small flat was sometimes as busy as a beehive. People were constantly coming in and out, chatting, joking, drinking coffee and brandy, watching TV, making love, while money passed from hand to hand. In time, however, fewer and fewer people visited Milija. There were a number of reasons for that. First, many of his friends, men of his age, died. Second, the amount of 'young blood' decreased drastically after the disintegration of the former Yugoslavia. An especially great loss resulted from the war in Bosnia, since the majority of young guys came from there, and most of them were Muslims. Now they stopped coming to Belgrade and those who lived here either went home or fled abroad. Handsome blond Enes and Fahro live in Italy where they earn money, like in Belgrade, through prostitution. Edin is in Hamburg where he works as a cook in a fish restaurant. Suad who used to write beautiful poetry — he gave me some — lives in Vienna now, where he works as a manual labourer. I heard that he suffered from nostalgia and has taken up heavy drinking. Azir stayed in the Muslim enclave of Srebrenica. Milija sent a parcel to him through the Red Cross. I don't know what became of Asmir, a beautiful young man who had a strong fabulous body, who could kiss so beautifully, do a blow job and screw without any feeling of guilt an all in a very manly way.

I haven't heard of Senel either, a dark-haired boy I met at the railway station, with whom I had one of the most exciting sexual adventures in my life. He seemed like a hoodlum, so I rented a room at the Hotel Astoria. We drank and made love the whole night long. Nobody turned me on like he did. We saw each other again a couple of times after that. I paid him every time even though he enjoyed it so much. The guy liked my Swatch so I gave it him as a farewell present. Milija said that he'd joined the Muslim army and he now kills Serbs. I can't believe it. I wonder if he still wears my Swatch. Of the Muslim boys only Samir and Soni stayed in Belgrade. They both still go to Milija's place despite the fact that the old man is sometimes seized by an anti-Muslim hysteria, when he decides to 'throw all Muslims out of his place because they kill Serbs!' Such 'patriotic' decisions do not last long — whenever he is hot or discovers a new Muslim guy with a big cock, he contradicts his own principles. Once he threw Samir out of his flat because he was Muslim, while at the same time Soni used to go there to fuck him. When I pointed out the illogicality of his actions he said that "Soni has a big, thick prick!" It was a strong argument. I couldn't contradict him.

The third reason why people stopped going to Milija's 'salon' was that he was getting intolerant and grumpy. He started quarrelling with many of his friends over quite banal things or for some completely invented and silly reasons. He also decided to stop inviting a great number of younger guys, some of them because they were Muslims or Albanians, some because they were rude and impolite, some because they drank, smoked or ate too much when they came to his place, some because they were thieves and bad guys, some because they were 'fags' or 'sissies', or because they just watched TV, or because they came too seldom etc., etc. — the list of reasons were endless. For all these reasons then, the number frequenting Milija's nowadays is very small. I am one of the few he didn't throw out and who still go there. At the same time, I became the main supplier of the 'salon', still bringing 'fresh merchandise' directly from the railway station. It is probably one of the reasons he hasn't yet thrown me out. On the other hand I prefer to take suspicious or dangerous-looking guys there. Our mutual interest strengthens our friendship.

★★★

The meaning of Milija's life, like my own, lies in the field of sex. It was the link that connected us during the ten years of our companionship. He had his first sexual intercourse when he was fourteen, in his home village somewhere in the south of Serbia. He was encountered by a large peasant on a road while coming back from school. He pushed him up against a fence — the original fence! — took his shorts off, spat in his hand, lubricated him and shoved his cock into Milija's arse. Milija said that the peasant only put the tip of his cock in. He fled his village when he was sixteen and went to Belgrade. To start with he worked as an apprentice in a clothes shop. As he says, he was 'young and handsome'. This is true, I have seen his photographs. He made love with older guys only for some favour, money or gifts. For instance he received a piece of English cloth for trousers from the owner of the shop. He did it with young guys for pleasure, he used to buy them drinks and later he started paying them. He still has a large collection of photographs of his ex-lovers. Most of them were really handsome.

He says that life before the Second World War was really okay and that he had a lot of sexual adventures or 'cases' as he puts it. The police weren't strict and didn't particularly pursue gays. Thanks to a man who worked as head waiter at the hotel Srpska Kruna, who fell in love with him, he got a job as a junior waiter. At the time, it was the best hotel in Belgrade so he earned well thanks to the tips. He also told me of a great scandal when the head waiter took cutlery and plates from the hotel for his private gay party.

Looking for missing things the police rushed into his apartment in the middle of the night only to find a group of men dressed as women there. It was said that there were some very respectable people there. A satirical magazine wrote about it later.

During the War things went well for Milija. He was living better then than now. He continued working as a waiter, but started selling things on the black market. He smuggled sausage, flour and other goods from Vojvodina. Of course, he seduced enemy soldiers. He says he fucked German soldiers and was fucked by Italians. He remembers with great pleasure beautiful Hans, a member of the Afrika Korps, who came to Belgrade for vacation. He was blond and sun-tanned. Milija met him at a café where he worked. He invited him for a drink or something and after they'd got drunk they went to bed. Milija lay beside him trembling from passion and fear — he wanted so badly to make love with the guy but he was afraid since the German had a pistol and a machine-gun which were on the chair together with his clothes. Nevertheless, he gained courage and started touching the guy's cock noticing that it was already stiff. The German turned round and they started kissing and caressing each other passionately. He spent a wild night with him and says he fucked him several times — it sounds a bit like 'patriotic bragging' to me! Hans gave him a photograph of himself wearing uniform. After the war when the Communists came to power Milija destroyed the photo because he was afraid it might be found during a possible search of his flat.

He also remembers a dark-haired, manly Italian, Giovanni. That fascist soldier screwed him several times during the occupation. He was gallant and often brought cigarettes, drink, food and similar things to Milija. After the War this Italian soldier was captured by partisans and shot.

Milija went on with his sexual activities with the same intensity. Immediately after liberation, his life was endangered. He met a drunk and armed Russian soldier. He promised the man he would find him a girl for sex. They went to a dark park where the girl was supposed to be waiting. While they were waiting. Milija started touching the Russian guy and when the latter got a hard-on Milija stooped to give him a blow job. At that moment the soldier started and began shouting. Milija jumped to his feet and ran as fast as he could. The Russian took out his gun and chased after him shouting, "I'll kill you! I'll kill you!" Fortunately he was so drunk he couldn't catch up with Milija. He just shot into the air. Since then Milija has hated Russians. He says the German occupiers were better than the Russian liberators. Unlike Germans, who were 'polite and decent', Russians were 'crude and drunk' and they took anything they wanted, they were especially fond of watches. He stayed away from Russians during the period when they were in Belgrade. He did not want to have any contact with them, he hated them from both an ideological and a nationalist viewpoint.

Shortly after the War, Milija was arrested by OZNA — the intelligence service — because of an chain of events which started during the War and finished after liberation. At the beginning of the occupation, Milija met a handsome bloke with a 'thick, fleshy cock', who fucked him a couple of times. The guy's name was Zdravko and he was from Sabac. First he was a chetnik, a member of the old National Guard and wore their uniform. Later Milija met him dressed in the uniform of the German *'Schutz'* police, together with another young man wearing the same uniform. The other guy was Croat and he had succeeded, using his connections, to get Zdravko into the German police force. Milija invited them for a drink and they had sex together. Later they all went to Šarić's, a photographer in Terazije Street, to have photographs taken. Milija knew the photographer since he was gay too. After that he never saw the two guys in German uniform again.

However during the winter of 1945, Zdravko appeared at Milija's door. Milija was amazed to see him wearing a partisan's uniform with a red star on his cap. He came together with his Croat friend, also in partisan uniform. They again had sex with Milija and spent several days together, going out to cafés, etc., but then Milija was taken into custody by OZNA. It was said that the warrant was signed by Slobodan Penezić Krcun, the chief of the secret police in person. During the interrogation inspectors showed him the photograph taken at Sarić's shop during the occupation, with Zdravko and his friend in German uniform. After identifying them and admitting everything he was taken to prison. He was released the next morning with orders to find Zdravko and his friend. He found them both in the café Kasina where they used to go together. OZNA agents arrested them there. Later Milija heard they'd been shot. It was much later that he found out why they were arrested and shot. Zdravko went with his companion to the photographer Šarić. They tied him up, beat him and stole his money and other valuable things. The vengeful photographer developed the negative with them wearing the two German uniforms and gave the photographs to OZNA. That was more than enough reason for being shot, collaborating with the enemy and robbery with violence.

Milija thinks that Šarić knew Krcun in person for a long time previously when they were Communists. He even thinks that Šarić, being rich, paid Krcun for sexual favours when the latter was a poor student. If it hadn't been so, Šarić wouldn't have dared reveal his own homosexual preference through the photograph given to OZNA, which was very dangerous during this period of Communist puritanism. Milija felt very sorry about Zdravko. He says it was 'a great shame' — if Zdravko had a small dick it would have been 'a small shame'. He, of course blames the 'sissy' Šarić for everything.

The other great affair was less dramatic but Milija stayed for more than a year in prison because of it. He managed to seduce a young officer of the Yugoslav National Army from Montenegro who came occasionally to Belgrade staying at Milija's. The officer sent two of his friends there for a night. Milija tried to persuade them both to have sex with him. It was the one who didn't sleep with him 'the Montenigrin bastard' who reported the whole thing to his garrison headquarters. An investigation took place, the officers admitted everything and were dismissed from the army. Milija was arrested and sentenced to one year and five months in prison. They also took away the "large beautiful apartment I owned on Nušić Street". Then he started hating Communists and Tito. He often repeats that he went to prison for fucking with Tito's officers. He still has a photograph of the first officer. He says that he met him several times after the whole affair. Afterwards the guy got married and had two kids. Now he lives with his family in Zadar.

When Milija was released from prison, where he'd had 'a good time' with some prisoners, and even with a guard, he took a job as a waiter in the Madera restaurant. He didn't stay there for long — as soon as an opportunity arose he moved to Paris with some friends. He spent three years there having a great time. He still receives a French pension which enables him to live quite comfortably in Belgrade. He spends money on young men and on trips. When he returned from Paris, he again took a job as a waiter at various cafés. He used to take young men there and buy them drinks, and seduce male customers. Every time his colleagues discovered he was gay, he changed his working place. In order to stop the rumours that he was gay, he sometimes slept with waitresses and female cooks. He says he fucked them so well that they bragged about it at work saying that such a good fucker couldn't possibly be gay. From time to time he had jobs at cafés on the Montenegrin coast. There he also had a lot of 'cases', which he proves by a heap of old photographs showing him with athletic young men in bathing suits.

★★★

Milija is a typical example of a 'bright and cunning old peasant'. He is uneducated, has numerous prejudices, but he always finds his way through. He uses most of his cunning for getting young men, for getting as much money as he can from everything and for overcoming the difficulties of life. It is impossible to list all the dramatic episodes in his life. For example, a guy who was a regular at his place drugged him by putting pills in his glass of milk. When the old man went to sleep, the guy stole the keys out of his pocket, and went off with 1,600 US dollars, jewellery, old Serbian army medals from the First World War earned by Milija's father and some other valuable objects from a drawer. Milija felt dizzy for two days after the event, partly because of the pills, partly because of the shock he went through. He was brave enough to report the whole thing to the police, which other homosexuals rarely do out of fear of compromising themselves. The investigation made no progress, they couldn't trace the thief so Milija decided to find him on his own. He made several enquiries and found out that the guy, a Muslim by the way (important if we are to understand the deepness of Milija's hatred) was hiding at the place of a man called Žika, whose nickname was Žaklina, who was also gay and a thief specialising in stealing valuable ikons from churches. Milija told the police about the thief's location and he was easily caught, together with Žaklina.

When the trial started Milija was summoned several times as the damaged party. In the court the thief and Milija accused each other of being faggots. Milija even said in rage, "Yes, I'm a faggot, but I'm a man. I fucked you in the arse, you Muslim sissy! You bandit scum!" I can imagine the judge's face and the faces of the jury. The thief got eighteen months for that. Milija wasn't satisfied, so he started saying that the woman judge liked the accused and probably fucked with him. When the guy was released from prison, he met Milija at the Moskva hotel. They made an arrangement that Milija should pay for the rest of his father's medals. He wanted me to be present at that transaction. The exchange of money and medals was performed very swiftly and coldly. They both stood because Milija had not invited him to sit. Nevertheless I wouldn't be surprised if he renewed his love relations with the 'Muslim sissy' and 'bandit scum' one day. Having in mind the great numbers of thieves, cheats, rascals, bandits and even murderers who stayed at his place, it can be said that he has had a lot of luck in his life.

One of the funnier episodes involved a tall blond guy called Dejan, who had one of the biggest pricks I've ever seen. One afternoon he was at Milija's, sitting and watching TV. When the old man went to sleep on his couch, Dejan got up, took a piece of ham Milija had brought up from the country and hid it in his sleeve or inside his jacket. When Milija woke up, Dejan said he had to go. It was much later in the evening, when old Milija opened his refrigerator intending to have dinner, that he noticed the ham was gone. I couldn't help laughing when he told me of the event.

Dejan was arrested later. He and one of his friends — a

gay man I know from the railway station, he tried to seduce me a couple of times — used to rob foreign-currency dealers, mostly Albanians, on Francuska Street. They used to tell them they were from the police. The other guy even wore a uniform he borrowed from his brother-in-law, a real policeman. Dejan also used to rob gays in the park at Ušće. When they were arrested their photos were shown on TV and in the papers along with information on what they had done. Milija and I were amazed when we saw the photo of his paid lover on TV. When he was released, he volunteered for Serb paramilitary units in Bosnia — I think they were the units of the 'duke' Šešelj — probably moved by the wish to rape, rob, and get rich in the easiest way. It seems he paid for his wish with his life. He hasn't been around since, and we heard that he'd been killed. I must go see his mother, who works as a lavatory cleaner at Hotel Slavija, to find out what exactly happened to Dejan.

★★★

Milija also had great troubles connected with a murder in Belgrade. An elderly homosexual, chief cook at the canteen of a construction enterprise, was found dead in his apartment. The man went occasionally to Milija's and took boys to his place. After some investigation the police began to get some idea of what was going on over at Milija's flat. They invited all the young men that used to go there all the clients, including me, for a 'chat' at the station. They were pretty polite, I can't complain. They told me they didn't want to interfere in my private life and they were only interested in facts important for the case which might help them find the murderers. I told them all I knew and they didn't contact me again. However Milija was called back several times and even threatened because they felt he was covering up for the murderer. He spent one whole night in jail, and, as it seems, it was then that they broke into his apartment and searched it.

Milija was very shocked by this affair. Eventually they arrested a guy named Sulja, a sweet little Albanian aged seventeen. It was me who'd picked him up at the railway station and taken him to Milija's. Fingerprints showed that Sulja visited the murdered person, which was the reason for them to make him a suspect. When his mother heard this she committed suicide. Later, Sulja turned out to be innocent, so they let him go. The real murderers were found much later. They were two workers from the construction company where the man worked. They knew he was a homosexual and abused his weakness, killed him cruelly — it was even said that they'd chopped off parts of his body — and robbed him.

A year ago, Milija had a traffic accident. He ran across the street near his house. Instead of using an underground passage he liked to run across the street at this dangerous crossing. Once, when he was going back home after dinner at the Kolarac restaurant, a big black car hit him. It knocked him down, dragged him several metres, and then ran away. Milija was left lying unconscious and covered with blood. He had concussion, and thighbone and upper arm fractures. The skin on his leg was almost completely torn. He was taken into the emergency ward and then to the Orthopaedic Hospital in Banjica. Everybody thought he would die, if not from the fractures then from having to lie still for all that time. They were wrong, the old man survived. After being hospitalised for three months, and spending one more month in a spa, he returned home completely cured.

He then discovered that his grandson had destroyed all the photographs with naked young men and that he had prepared one of his photos for an obituary. That made him so furious — he couldn't forgive him for destroying photos of his lovers, among which were some very vulgar ones. He even shouted that he would cut him out of his will. After that he calmed down and now and then has good relations with his grandson. Six months after being released from hospital he decided to have an operation on his hernias. He put up with this problem for years and the hernias got larger making normal sex impossible. I persuaded him to have an operation as soon as possible.

He was released five days after the operation. Doctors tried to persuade him to stay a few more days because he was old, but he would have none of it. His reason for haste was that he'd had a row with a nurse, I don't know why. He went home by taxi on his own. I am always amazed at his energy. At the age of eighty, he can have sex like a young man. He brought a bottle of whisky to the doctor who performed the operation and thanked him "for giving me back my manliness".

Milija is not afraid of death like I am. He fulfilled his life with the thing he loved most — men. He never had doubts about what he was doing, but did the things he found right and proper. His simple nature never asked any questions about the meaning of certain activities and life in general. He always stood firmly on the ground and only observed things around himself. He never looked toward the skies — sometimes I wonder if he is aware of what death really means. Is he aware of the tragedy of nothingness, of going back to the eternal non-existence? He doesn't care! He thinks only of the problems connected to the everyday world: his pension, price of electricity, refrigerator repair, why his friend Saša didn't tell him that he'd met a new boy from Kraljevo, why he couldn't get a hard-on when he wanted to sleep with Samir yesterday, why a butcher sold him half-rotten minced-meat, etc., He knows death is near, but he is completely absorbed in everyday life, as if death was completely irrelevant. A long time ago, he had a crypt built for himself in his native village. He has a photograph of himself standing beside his future grave. His name and date of birth are already engraved on a marble stone. The only empty space on it is left for the date of death. Everything is ready for his arrival.

February 23rd, 1993

Police Interrogation

Željko called me today. He told me a story which shocked me. The other day two plainclothes inspectors took him to the police station for a chat about his part in a talk show dedicated to the position of homosexuals in Serbia on the privately owned radio station Penguin. First he refused to go with them because they didn't have an arrest warrant. And then they told him they would arrest him anyway for listening to fascist songs — he was listening to a cassette by the Croat singer Radojka Šverko. They took him to the main precinct on 29th November Street and interrogated him for a few hours. They wanted him to give them the names of all members of Arcadia — the first, though still illegal gay rights association in Belgrade.

In all the hurry he forgot to tell me if he'd divulged the names, including my own, or not. We made a date to see each other at Srdjan's place on Friday, at a meeting of Arcadia. The news shocked and scared me. Every day there was a possibility that the police would knock at my door. As they are allowed to get away with almost anything and are awfully crude and primitive, they might arrest me and then harass me, humiliate, beat or blackmail me. That makes my decision to leave everything and go abroad even firmer. I am aware that it would be a difficult step, as I'd probably be lonely and nostalgic there — wherever that might be — but at least I would not be constantly afraid of getting arrested.

★★★

February 26th, 1993

I went to Srdjan's place, to the meeting of Arkadia. Željko told us all the details about what happened at the police precinct. After they took him in for interrogation, they beat him with batons all over his body, telling him to give all the names of the members of our association. Despite all this he did not give away any names. I was shocked, but I didn't find anything strange about it any more. Everything is possible in this country, where anarchy rules along with organised crime. Highest officials of the domestic mafia are MPs in the parliament, where they pretend to be ardent patriots — although they have already drawn their salary as 'patriots' through robberies and war profits. The police prefer harassing homosexuals to chasing thieves and criminals. That is not so strange because homosexuals are easy to arrest and molest, whereas criminals are dangerous, so common policemen are afraid of them, respect them and admire them. Moreover there seems to be a very successful collaboration between the police and organised crime at all levels. I often see cops and black-market money dealers chatting very friendly and confidentially with each other, giving each other money secretly and so on. It seems that we are doomed, this country is ruled by ex-communists and nationalists who manage to persuade the uneducated nation with the help of the media that they are the greatest patriots who defend the Serb nation and its interests. I don't see any way out — I have to flee!

April 26th, 1993

Coloured Petrol

The Bosnian Serbs rejected the Vance-Owen peace plan, despite Milošević, Ćosić and Bulatović insisting they accept it. Even stricter sanctions are to be imposed on Yugoslavia from today. I'm afraid that from now on there won't be any petrol to buy, not even as much as they manage to smuggle in from other countries — which must be the most expensive petrol in the world. If the West closes the frontiers of Yugoslavia completely, I will have to reduce going everywhere by car as well as my cruising. Although there hasn't been any petrol at filling stations for some time we managed to get it somehow or other.

First I had my own suppliers, whom I ordered from by phone, then there have been smugglers on every corner, in car parks, in the street, etc. selling petrol. They can be recognised by plastic Coke bottles full of petrol placed in front of their cars, in which they keep buckets filled with the fuel. Thus I learned that petrol comes in various colours. Earlier, while petrol was available at filling stations, I didn't pay any attention to its colour. Now I've found out that the best kind of petrol comes from Greece and is a light green colour. Hungarian petrol, 'Shell'-oil they call it, which is also high quality, is red. Romanian petrol is the worst kind, it is as yellow as urine and smells of gas. There is also petrol from the Ukraine available on the black market coming in from Albania and imported by boats over Lake Skutari. Of course, smugglers who sell petrol mix it and make cocktails, adding green or red colour to make it look like the more expensive kind. They also often mix the stuff with oil, gas or water. Therefore our cars increasingly malfunction and often can't be turned off because they are filled with gas.

Filters are often blocked, valves burn, but people keep on driving.

★★★

Nikola told me the other day that a gay boy was killed in Ušće Park. When he described him to me, I remembered who he was. When I saw his photo in newspaper obituaries, I was positive it was the guy I knew by sight. I was never introduced to him formally, and I didn't know his name. From the obituary I found out his name was Neša and he was from Niš. Nikola told me he studied English language and literature at the University. I saw him occasionally in the railway station toilets and at Staklenac. Most of the time, he liked to stand at a urinal in a corner and wank his big cock, which was completely out of proportion to his willowy slim body. He would cast nervous glances around at the same time. He was tall and thin. He wore his long blond hair tied back in a pony-tail. He wore casual clothes, but he had style. I saw him mostly wearing a wide light-coloured coat, always with a small black rucksack on his shoulders. I also used to see him on Prince Mihajlo Street with some girls, probably colleagues from the University. Once I even followed him and approached him, trying to start a conversation. He ignored me completely, he went past me, not paying any attention to my questions and making an arrogant face. That hurt me. I was so unattractive to him that he didn't want to say one word to me. He could at least show me he wasn't interested in a polite way, not like that.

I disliked him from that moment on. I began to see his bad side and concluded that he was an empty-headed conceited sissy amongst other things. He always strutted as if he was the Prince of Wales. I noticed too that he never seemed to talk with anyone from gay circles. I thought it must have stemmed from guilt about being homosexual which often happens with students from provincial towns. He probably thought he could run away from himself by avoiding other gays. Such frustrated guys always get on my nerves. They want to hide their gayness from themselves and from others although the fact is quite obvious. His appearance was quite conspicuous, not only because he was tall and blond but also because he moved effeminately when he walked. That probably betrayed him in the park. His assassins probably discovered he was gay quite easily. The poor guy, he wasn't even aware of his appearance. Besides, he was a beginner, he wasn't familiar enough with the dangerous places in Belgrade, so he wasn't able to take care of himself, to sense danger coming and to run off. If he'd talked with other gays more often he'd have probably learnt something useful and perhaps have even saved his life.

I will have to be quite careful in the next few weeks. The police will most likely begin taking homosexuals into custody as usual, gathering them from their cruising places for interrogation. They always do that although they must be aware that homosexuals almost never kill their fellows, since they all have similar problems. By the way, gay murders happen at regular intervals, approximately one every other year. The murderers can't be that easily discovered because they usually don't know their victims before the fatal encounters. Therefore it is difficult to find clues or any sort of link which connects the felon with his victim. Finally one usually has the impression that the police don't do their best to solve such cases. They don't care much for faggots.

In the afternoon I was supposed to meet Brana in front of the British Council Library to give him a new porn video. On the corner of Nikola Spasić and Prince Mihajlo Street there was a cute boy I had noticed long before, sitting on the edge of a street flower-pot. He wore baggy jeans and a pair of shiny brown cowboy boots. He had on a grey jacket and underneath a black roll-neck sweatshirt. He had a beautiful face and his hair was short. He walked in a straight and dignified manner, like a young deer. He was aware of his beauty — there was a flair of superiority in his appearance. I had often seen him in Staklenac. He never stood for long at the urinals. Several times I tried to catch up with him on his way out of the toilets. I even managed to approach him once, when I asked him, "Sorry, what's the time?" He replied somewhat rudely — I can't remember what he said. I looked at him now, passing beside him and he surprisingly looked back at me. I didn't hope for anything having in mind my previous experience with him. I went on my way, not looking back.

When I stood to look in the window of Naućna Knjiga bookshop, I noticed he'd caught up with me and was now in front. He walked slowly, stopping in front of every shop window. This time he wasn't rushing as usual. That gave me some hope and I started following him. He of course noticed, but he didn't hurry. That was a good sign. He went into the passage near the Cinephoto shop. Then he stopped in front of the Domaća Radinost shop window. He continued out of the passage slowly and turned right towards Tanjug. He was walking more and more slowly. I decided I had to do something soon otherwise he might get fed up with me following him and with my indecisiveness. I summoned up the courage and approached him. The first questions are often the most stupid ones but everything depends on them. I asked him where he was from, I was a little afraid he'd answer rudely again but no, he answered in a very polite manner, with a smile on his face, "From Novi Beograd, Block Sixty-one." I told him we were neighbours. I then asked him which school he attended but he wasn't telling. He simply said, "Never mind!" He seemed pretty suspicious and I was discouraged, but nevertheless I did invite him over to my place and much to my surprise he accepted. I was overwhelmed with joy. He said he didn't have that much time as he had to be at Republic Square at seven-thirty. I promised to give him a lift back as we walked to my car.

On the way he was very quiet and self-absorbed though he did tell me his name was Alexander and that he intended to study dentistry at the University and to move abroad somewhere after graduating (I never understand people who want to be dentists for anything other than money). On arrival at my flat he removed his new shiny boots. He went into my living-room and looked over my books, cassettes and CDs. I offered him some juice or vodka, but he refused both. Perhaps he thought I might poison him or give him a sleeping draft. I sat down beside him and tried to begin a conversation. However the boy was so uncommunicative that all my efforts failed. Irritated, I gave up trying. I decided to speed up the whole thing, so I started kissing him on the cheek and neck. He was wearing an exquisite perfume resembling Missoni. He turned his head away when I tried kissing his lips. I was unsure whether it was fear of AIDS or simply that he wasn't into kissing. We stripped each other gradually and when down to our underwear lay down on my bed. We caressed for a while then he took off my underpants. He stroked my cock, squeezed it and wanked me. He stared at my big prick as if it was the first time he'd ever seen an erect cock — or at least a cock of that size. He played with my dick for a long time looking at it from all sides as if it was a rare and exotic animal. At one moment he was squeezing so hard it hurt. I told him not to squeeze it so hard and to be more gentle, adding that it wasn't a rubber dildo.

After that he started sucking and licking it. The 'obscure object of his desire' was, after so much hesitation, finally inside his mouth. He held it firmly while he was giving me a blow job, as if he was afraid it might get away. He was looking me in the eyes all the time, trying to catch every change in my expression. I didn't like it because I couldn't concentrate. I wasn't able to relax and enjoy looking at his beautiful head into which my cock was disappearing. He interrupted his sucking several times to catch breath, then went on as violently as before. Then the phone rang.

It was Brana, calling to say how angry he was because I hadn't kept my date at the agreed time to give him the video I'd promised earlier. I told him that a 'higher power' prevented me, and he understood immediately what I meant. While I was talking with Brana the boy ran off into the bathroom. He was standing in front of the toilet, wanking. He went down on his knees and started sucking my cock again, wanking himself simultaneously. At the very moment when I began to come and ejaculate in his mouth, he jumped off. He turned towards the toilet and wanked off into it. I had never met such a clean and neat boy. He didn't want us to make the bed sheets dirty with our sperm so he discharged his load into the toilet. Maybe his mother had shouted at him for leaving stains on his sheets when he'd had wet dreams. Maybe he was so frustrated because of that he could never have an orgasm in bed. After we'd showered he asked me for a mouthwash. I poured some Odol liquid into a glass of tepid water. He gargled for a long time. Before we left I put down my telephone number on a piece of paper for him. As promised I took him to Republic Square.

June 28th, 1993

Neighbour Djoka

After my uncle's death, aunt Zita wanted to exchange her flat in Karaburma for a smaller one in the centre. She was looking for a flat near Palilula open-air market because her daughter lived in the neighbourhood. After a long and fruitless search, in which I helped, we managed to find a place which suited her. The flat was on March 27th Street, in one of two high-rises next to the market place. It was fortunately on the second floor, so it wasn't difficult for her to climb the stairs when the lift was out of order, which happens often in such buildings. A family of four lived in the apartment. The father was Djoka, a worker at the engine factory in Rakovica, the mother was Verica, a clerk at the post office, and they had two little kids — a boy of seven and a girl of nine.

The place was furnished with cheap kitschy furniture, cupboards with ornamental bands on them, which made them look like coffins, the usual red couch with two armchairs, goblins in gold-dyed plaster frames, a winter landscape probably taken from a calendar. In the corridor above a door to one of the rooms there was a framed picture of 'duke' Šešelj. When my aunt saw that she said jokingly that she didn't want to take the flat because of the picture. From our conversation we concluded that Djoka was a great supporter of the right Radical Party, and even a president of a local committee or something like that. He and his wife were moreover from the Serb Krajina in Croatia, a village near Knin. He was a simple-minded primitive person, whereas she was more educated and intelligent. They both concealed their peasant cunning with their 'frankness' and 'sincerity'. After several visits, detailed examinations of flats and conversations they finally decided they wanted to exchange flats.

The whole administrative procedure — obtaining papers from the court, the communal assembly and the ministry — took almost two months. After that period they finally moved.

Djoka phoned my aunt the other day to tell her that some letters and bills had come to her old address. She asked me to go and fetch the letters. I felt too lazy to go there for days. I knew I would lose at least one hour through having to listen to their stories and having coffee and brandy. I finally decided to go today. First I announced my visit on the phone. When I arrived Djoka was repairing the balcony door. The place was still in a mess, the floors were covered in rolls of carpet, scattered chairs etc. He was alone in the flat while his wife was at work, one of the kids at school the other playing in front of the building. He offered me a cup of coffee and some brandy. I told him I was in a hurry to make a lunch date, but he nevertheless made some coffee, so I had to drink it. I told him I didn't drink alcohol, so he poured me a glass of cranberry juice. He talked about some unimportant things I can't even remember now. In due course I showed him the telephone bill my aunt had paid for him. He said he didn't have enough money for it because he was out of work due to the economic sanctions. His monthly income was no more than twenty-five deutschmark. He had only half the amount on him, which he gave to me, apologising.

Then he suddenly said that he'd fuck a faggot for twenty marks. I don't know why he said that. I thought at the time that it was a coincidence. However, a couple of minutes later, he said he had talked with his colleagues from work about for how much money they would sleep with a homo for. They said they'd do it for a hundred mark. However, he thought they lied and that they would do it for ten or twenty. I was just smiling and nodding but didn't say anything. I tried to divert the conversation to different topics, but unsuccessfully. I came to realise that he wasn't talking about gays accidentally. It was obvious that he had a plan in his mind. That became clear when he said, half-joking, that when he was young he fucked men if they paid for his lunch or dinner. He slept with a guy from his town, who studied in Belgrade. In the meantime the guy graduated and got a job as a clerk in the Federal Administration. The guy took Djoka to the famous singer Zdravko Čolić, where they drank foreign whisky.

As a young man he was quite successful with girls too, although he wasn't very beautiful, perhaps because he had a big cock — he probably wanted to turn me on by such bragging! Nevertheless since he got married he realised that all women were witches and vipers. He said this friend of his, the faggot, was right when he advised him not to get married. It was definitely clear to me at this point that his stories about gays were intentional and that he wanted to achieve something with them. He probably guessed I was one and wanted to let me know that I could have him for twenty deutschmark or a meal. I pretended not to get his message. He offered me more coffee, but I refused. He asked me to stay to lunch, but I told him I had to go to my mother's. He even wanted to play a game of chess with me, but I said no.

Then I changed my mind. Why not take the opportunity, I thought. My philosophy is anyway like the song: "Take everything life offers, today you're a bud, tomorrow you're a faded flower," In my case this advice has even more ultimate meaning, as I'm a faded flower today and tomorrow a flower in a dustbin. I decided to accept his offer, not because I was turned on by Djoka — he was too old, hairy and ugly for my taste — but because the whole situation was exciting. He was a model father of a family, a good worker, a macho man from Krajina, a member of the Radical Party, etc. I'm at his place, at the same time in my aunt's ex-flat. Above all, one of his children was playing downstairs and the child, or the wife, could appear at the door at any moment. All that turned me on. I decided to play the game to the end. To make things more amusing I decided to play the role of a naive guy who'd never had homosexual intercourse. I waited for him to start talking about homosexuals again to start realising my scenario. I didn't have to wait long before Djoka started provoking me again with his homo adventures.

"I'll be fuckin' damned, Boris, if that fag friend of mine wasn't right when he said I should get rid of women. What's wrong with Zdravko Čolić?"

"Tell me are you kidding? Have you really fucked faggots?" I asked curiously, playing naive.

"Yes, let me drop dead if I'm lying!" he said loudly, following his words with a blow with his fist to his chest, which was supposedly an additional proof of his sincerity.

"What does it feel like? How did you like it?" I continued my game.

"Well... it wasn't bad. It's the same as screwing a chick."

"Did they give you blow jobs?"

"Yes! The motherfuckers give better blow jobs than women!"

I had the impression that this statement was sincere, so I decided to reveal my cards.

"Know what? I've never had such an experience. I just jacked off once with a buddy during my high-school days. I've often thought about it. I'd like to try," I said in a confidential tone, trying to look as sincere and naive as possible.

"You'd like to fuck a faggot?"

"No, no, it doesn't have to be a faggot, and I don't have to fuck him, I'd just like to try it with a man who would show me how it is done."

"Well, the best thing would be to introduce you to that friend of mine. He's experienced in those things, and he's also well-educated."

"No, I'm not interested in a notorious faggot. I don't want to be with men like him. I have a girlfriend. I just want to try it once with a man and that's all. Just to see what it looks like..."

"Aah, well... I don't know." By the expression on his face, I could tell he was beginning to see what I wanted, but didn't dare say it aloud. I decided to help him. We were close to the dramatic point in our conversation.

"Perhaps you could show me what it looks like? Maybe you could do to me the things you did to him. What do you say?" The die was cast.

"Well... What the hell! Okay!" he said, smiling.

"Let's start then. Tell me what I should do, I don't know."

I enjoyed this performance without an audience. We got up, and he started squeezing and pinching my arse. He opened his zip and took out a big thick cock which was half erect. He pushed my head down and said, "Suck it now!" First I sucked only its head, pretty unskilfully so that he wouldn't know it wasn't my first time. However, he shoved it deeper down my throat, so I had to suck it whole. Then he ordered me to get up and remove my trousers. I did that and he bent me over a kitchen chair — it was all going on in the kitchen — he wet my arsehole with some spit and started sticking his big cock in. It hurt so much I couldn't stand it. I asked, "Don't you have some skin cream or something?"

"Fuck, I don't!" Crude as he was, he didn't even have hand cream at home. It occurred to me that I might use some vegetable oil, but he would make me dirty with it all over, and probably leave stains on my trousers. I remembered the scene from *Last Tango in Paris*, where they use butter, but it would have been silly of me to use the butter eaten by his wife and children. Besides butter from the fridge is hard and frozen, so it wouldn't be of any use. I finally got an idea — shampoo. I remembered a weird guy whom I fucked with the help of hair shampoo. I asked him immediately, "Do you have any shampoo?" "Yeah, in the bathroom." He came back with the shampoo and spread some over my arsehole. It itched and burned a little, but his cock slid up my arse more easily. I didn't like him fucking me bent over the kitchen chair like that. He shoved it up me too suddenly, not giving me enough time to relax and open up gradually. Fortunately the bloke came quickly. He went to the bathroom, took the bottle of shampoo back and washed his cock. When he came back he was smiling.

"Well! How was it? What do you say?" he laughed.

"To tell you the truth, it hurt me. I didn't like it. It seems that I wasn't born to be a faggot. This was the first and last time. I won't do it anymore!" That was my final sentence in the performance.

I told him I was already late for lunch at my mother's, which was true, and that I had to go immediately. I don't know what was going on in his head. Maybe he thought I made love with him because I liked him. That, of course, wasn't true. I didn't like him at all. For me he was just an instrument for taking revenge on established morality, the institution of the family, the cult of the working class, the right-wing party, macho men from Krajina and the whole society. Regardless of the fact that he fucked me I felt like a winner. I managed to destroy the illusion of an idyllic family. If it wasn't for those things I would never have made it with him. But he will never be aware of that. Who knows, maybe by fucking me he also took his revenge on intellectuals in the name of the working class. Maybe I was just his tool to achieve something. If that were true it would be a real farce in my taste. We had sex not because of mutual attraction, but as tools for revenge on some invisible people and institutions. Great!

July 1st, 1993

This City Will Follow Me

I haven't kept up my diary for a long time. I simply didn't feel like writing, and I've also had my doubts — for God knows how long — about the meaning of such writing. Why, what and whom is it for? However, I resume writing without much thought. It would be a pity if I really stopped now that I've written so much.

Nothing special has happened in my private life in the meantime. Mostly I just go through the same everyday routine with feelings of meaningless and hopelessness. Going out every day and visiting stinking toilets in the hope that I will have some good sex or will find 'the love of my life'. A lot of missed opportunities to have sex or make friends. My old skill in man-hunting and bravery seems to be lost. Now I hesitate, I am afraid, I do not want to take any risks (and I read somewhere, 'no risk, no fun'). I feel like a mangy old cat that doesn't manage to meet as many young cats as before — as if all sources of joy and energy have dried up. The state I'm now in is somewhere between resignation, depression, and a fatalistic surrender to the meaningless of everyday life, hoping that something will change when I reach the bottom coupled with the realization of the total absurdity of this life.

But such a hope is totally tragicomic because I have already reached the bottom. I fight with the meaninglessness every day, and still I am unable to change anything. I see emigrating to Australia as the only way out. I cannot say if I really want this but I am so desperate that I do not know what else to do. I am trying to convince myself that going there is the only way for me to be saved. It is only important to run away as far as possible from this crazy country. Of course, it is much more difficult to run away from yourself, but that's exactly what I'm trying with this escape to Australia. I want to forget Cavafy's 'City': "You won't find a new country, you won't find new seas. This city will follow you. You will walk down the same streets..."

I want to go away without anything, just one suitcase, to forget everything, my whole past life. I want to make a complete change, to become a different person, to start a new life. That's my goal. But when I think about it and analyse it, it seems to me that I would feel even more lonesome and tragic there, knowing myself as I do. Here, I have a few friends at least, acquaintances and what's left of my family, whereas there I do not have anybody. No, I must not think about it. Thinking prevents you from being active. I have to leave. I don't want to repent one day over a missed opportunity. I could come back at any time.

I am afraid of AIDS as well. I hear more and more frequently that someone has become infected or that someone has died. Brana told me that Dr K. had a lung cancer operation. Although he smoked a lot everyone thinks it was AIDS he died of because he went to New York, Amsterdam and similar places and had lots of sex. I saw Cleopatra and Ophelia on the street the other day and they are both incredibly skinny like walking skeletons. Cleopatra has started to lose his hair too. When I passed him he nodded and smiled in a sad and bitter way. His eyes and face had the expression of someone who is petrified with the terror of facing death. It's also said that Lajoš from Novi Sad got infected. He had a long affair with the late Žarko who recently died of AIDS. N. is another person who's lost a lot of weight recently.

I too have lost five or six kilograms since last year. All my trousers have become too large for me so I've had to buy new ones. I eat as much as I can, even took Biomed 6, a medical preparation for gaining weight, but I simply cannot put on any weight. I weigh myself every day hoping to have gained a couple of grams, always afraid that meanwhile I've lost more weight. I've stabilised at between sixty-five and sixty-six kilograms. Now I have convinced myself that the fact that I have lost five kilograms is not important, that it is the tendency that counts and that the important thing is to stop losing any more weight. I am happy that the loss has stopped now and I am trying not to go below sixty-five kilos — that would be a sign that there really were reason to panic. I am afraid to take the HIV test again.

The most dramatic event on the political front was the imprisonment of Vuk and Danica Drašković, the leader of the Serb Renewal Movement, the biggest opposition party, and his wife. I was there, in the demonstration in front of Parliament on the night it happened. Fortunately I left when the riots started so nothing happened to me. The cops threw tear gas and chased participants all over the centre of town. People were beaten up, even innocent passers-by. There were many wounded. Vuk, Danica and other representatives of the Serb Renewal Movement were arrested at their party's main office. A large group of special forces in camouflage clothes and bullet-proof vests and helmets carrying machine-guns raided the premises and arrested the leaders. They beat up Vuk and Danica, pulled their hair, knocked them down and kicked them on the way to the police van. In the van, and later in prison, they continued to beat them mercilessly. According to some reports, even Vuk's anus was injured.

The totalitarian tradition of physical and mental torture continues, the ultimate goal being the complete moral degradation and cruel destruction of all human dignity. With this case of violence, the present government removed its last democratic mask but unfortunately many people here are unwilling to see its true face. Nothing remains of the illusory 'democratic' state the people fought for. This is one of the darkest police regimes. I think of the beatings and humiliations the Drašković's underwent as a personal offence done to me and my own humiliation. I identified with them completely.

I wonder if this regime is aware of the hatred it arouses by torturing and humiliating the leader of the biggest opposition party and his wife. They were kept in separate cells, not allowed to communicate with each other and although seriously injured were not allowed proper medical treatment. It was only after great pressure was asserted on the government from the country at large and from abroad that they were allowed medical treatment, but again in separate rooms and heavily guarded. Police forces moreover guarded the whole floor and the building and no one was allowed in.

The state television hides all information concerning Vuk's time in prison, his health and the protests for his release. Vuk wrote a very dramatic message to the public in which he announced his hunger strike. I really don't know if he meant it or not. Even these dramatic events were not enough to make the whole opposition unite and move this inert and stultified people, still bewitched by official propaganda. Most people still believe that the distastrous situation in the country is a result of an 'international plot', a conspiracy by some great dark Serbophobic force, which hates Serbs not only because they are Slav and Orthodox but because they are a 'chosen' and 'heavenly' people with a special position in the world. Besides which common people blame the opposition for not having enough patriotic feeling, always complaining about things and making the situation even more confused, which makes things even more difficult to solve our problems and create a country which will cover all Serb territories.

July 5th, 1993

A Welding Torch

I had a very exciting day today, although I had some very boring business to do at the city hall and in a lawyer's office this morning, concerning the registration of my firm. According to the new law no one is allowed to own a business if they have a job in a company owned by the state, while the sanctions against Yugoslavia are on. As my firm had no chance of survival in this disastrous situation, I decided to transfer it to my aunt and to keep my job at the Faculty.

This afternoon I went to the railway station. I stood in the toilet on a platform for a long time. A very handsome short-haired boy, who looked like an ordinary hoodlum, loitered in front of the booths and sinks. First I thought he was there just by chance, and then discovered he did want something. He went into a toilet booth, I tried to follow him in but he did not let me in and pushed the door from inside. Then he went out again and resumed moving around. Then I went into a booth. I left the door ajar on purpose and started masturbating. He stood in front of the door, looking at me from time to time, but he did not try to come in. At one moment he asked me if I had a lighter. It sounded very funny to me, completely outrageous and crazy. He sees me masturbating in the toilet, but nevertheless he asks me for a light. I replied, "Yes I do, come on in," although I had no lighter on me. He refused my proposal with an unintelligible sound. I could hear that someone in the corridor had given him a light.

I masturbated further, losing every hope that he would come in. However he did come in at last, with a cigarette in his hand. I saw a big bulge in his trousers. I tried to take it with one hand and to pull him closer with the other and kiss him. He refused me sharply, moving his hand. The sharp movement of his hand with a scornful and arrogant expression on his face which seemed to mean: 'Back off! Don't touch me, you slimy faggot!' He inhaled more smoke from his cigarette, then suddenly knelt down took my cock with his right hand and observed it for a while as if he wanted to estimate its value. Finally concluding, apparently, that it was the right length and breadth, he took it in his mouth. He sucked it skilfully and with great care, but at the same time with curt and energetic movements. He even licked my balls with great delight. He stopped sucking and stood up a couple of times to take puffs from his cigarette and then again stooped down to continue sucking. He would not allow me to touch him even for a moment. I came in his mouth. Then he stood up and said in a cold and dignified voice, "Get away from the door!" He went out, still holding his cigarette in his left hand. Things like that did not happen to me often. He sucked me wildly but didn't allow me to touch him. Isn't that a contradiction? What was going on in his head? What does he think about all this?

I went out and took a short walk around the railway station, and then went back to the public toilet. A short dark-haired guy stood in front of a booth. We exchanged glances. He went into the booth and I followed him. We caressed for a while and then he sucked my cock. We had an orgasm masturbating each other. When I went out I saw a large, well-built short-haired guy go out from the next-door booth. He wore a pair of blue bermuda shorts and a multicoloured shirt. I recognised him as the guy I saw yesterday in the bus depot toilets. Our eyes met in the mirror above the sink while we were washing our hands. I did not dare approach him because he seemed too dangerous. Later I saw him sitting with Neša in a café — I'd been having sex with Neša for a long time so it was obvious to me that the guy was 'one of us'. It suddenly occurred to me that he might be the famous guy from Krajina — the subject of many legends in gay circles all over Belgrade. He went out of the toilet and stopped in front of a burger kiosk.

First I hesitated for a bit, but then I approached him and asked him a stupid question, something like, "Do you know how much a juice costs?" He accepted the conversation smoothly. We stood in front of the toilet for about five minutes talking, and then he invited me for a drink. We found a table at an open-air restaurant in front of the bus depot. We sat there for almost two hours — it was him talking most of the time and I just chatted him up with my questions. He said he was from Banja Luka. He was a member of the special forces in the army of the Bosnian Serb Republic. He was married and had a one-year-old son. His elder brother had been killed in the war, and he himself was wounded a couple of times — he showed me the scars on his leg and belly.

As a member of the special forces he took part in numerous acts of sabotage on the territories held by enemy forces. He robbed or, as he called it, 'took' thousands of German marks, four kilograms of gold and jewellery, several cars and various other goods. He offered me a VW Golf III or any other car for only three or four thousand deutschmark. He could steal the car from a Muslim, or from a Serb who owed him something, by way of revenge. He arrested three beautiful Muslim girls. He took them to a villa in Banja Luka, which he rented and turned into a sort of brothel. Those three poor girls work for him as prostitutes, and even serve him when he feels like it.

Apart from that, he was involved in a suspicious business of smuggling gas and other articles in short supply. He said a fried of his, or rather an ex-friend, cheated him and took thirty-five thousand deutschmark from him. He left for Greece with the money to buy two cisterns of gas, but he never came back. He said that there are about thirty thousand Muslims still in Banja Luka, before the war there were some eighty thousand. They are not allowed to leave the town because they want to have some hostages in case UN or NATO forces decide to bomb the airport. In that case all the Muslims would be brought to the airport and serve as a 'living shield'. They raid Muslim homes whenever they feel like it. They take anything they fancy from the scared people who live in these homes —TV sets, VCRs, fridges, washing machines, furniture, food, etc.

The guy killed a lot of Muslims and Coats in various military actions. He slaughtered many of them personally. He showed me the ID papers of a member of the Croat army. The identity card, covered in plastic, had the name Ante Lovrenčić on it and a colour photograph of a young dark-haired lad of about twenty-three. He cut his throat with his own hand and keeps the document as a 'souvenir'. He showed me other photographs too. In one of them he was dressed in camouflage clothes and had a machine-gun in his hands, and a voguish pair of Rambo shades on his face. Two guys, dressed similarly, stood beside him. He also showed me photos of his father and brother. I got quite sick when he related how he'd tortured and killed a Muslim captive. He tied him with wire to a tree. Then he took a welding torch, scorched his prisoner and cut him slowly with fire. He eventually cut his skull in half.

What did the poor man feel when this monstrous criminal approached him with the welding torch in his hands? I cannot bear even the thought of what that horror must have been. Is it possible that one man is capable of doing such things to another? Doesn't the executioner is such situations think even for a single moment that he could find himself in the same position? What do such physical and mental tortures feel like, when death seems the only release? I was stunned for a moment. He probably noticed I was astounded because of the face I made. Instead of an excuse — not that there can be any excuses for such crimes — he told me laconically that he became a beast. "You're worse than a beast!" I thought, "you're a monster!" He then told me he had witnesses of what he did and that he would probably be tried as a war criminal after the war. Because of this he intends to enlist in the Foreign Legion, or in the special police forces in Kosovo. He said they needed people like him there. He just felt like killing Albanians, and he also heard they were rich and had a lot of gold and foreign money in their homes. He hoped that a war would break out there soon.

★★★

I cannot remember now everything he told me. My head was throbbing after that horrible story. I had already read in the newspaper about some of the scary crimes which had been committed in this war. But it was completely different to hear it from one of the criminals themselves. He talked about the throat-cutting and torturing with a great nonchalance. He seemed like a blasé sportsman, used to being a winner, who talks calmly about his successes on the football field and the defeats suffered by the opposing team. I could not understand the complete lack of mercy or sympathy in him. He felt no repentance or pangs of conscience. What sort of man was he? Is it possible that the incessant nationalist propaganda of the state media had really managed to provoke hatred towards Muslims and Croats to the extent that they are able to torture and murder people with no repentance whatsoever! The ruling blind nationalism created a social climate in which hatred towards the opposing sides is more than positive, and at the same time all means to destroy them and eliminate them have become 'legal'.

All the sides in this war have their criminals and murderers in their armies but none of them are willing to admit it. They all only report crimes committed by the other sides. All boundaries of humanity are exceeded. How short was the time needed to remove the thin layer of politeness and humanity from people! How fast they have become beasts! In fact calling them 'beasts' is a compliment for them and an insult to animals, and therefore quite inadequate. They are 'anti-human' — a negation of all cultural development and the painstaking building of humanity. They are a shame on the human race — a reminder than culture is a gentle plant that withers quickly, and that the forces of evil and 'vertigo' are always present, prepared to break out with all their might at any time.

The guy who was sitting beside me was a representative of these wild, irrational beings. I was so astounded and shocked that I could not hate him. To me, he seemed the embodiment of a cosmic evil I was not familiar with. I was too weak to speak. The criminal might become a policeman in Kosovo very soon, and start robbing and murdering Albanians. He might even be transferred to Belgrade when some demonstrations break out here, to beat disobedient people and opposition leaders. It is possible that no court of justice will ever get him and that he will remain unpunished for the crimes he committed. Isn't there a God to prevent such crimes. Can't he hear the cries of the slaughtered, the ripped, the dismembered and the scorched, of raped girls and old women? Let this guy be captured by enemy soldiers and cut to pieces by a welding machine. That would be the only fit punishment, although not strong enough. He would have to have as many lives as those he took, so that it would be possible for him to die in pain many times. I know that it is not Christian to seek revenge, but I really wonder if there is a normal person who would allow such a criminal to live. Unfortunately it seems that there are not many normal people here nowadays.

★★★

We changed the topic of our conversation after a short but unpleasant silent interval. He said that he had his first homosexual experience in the ex-Yugoslav army. He was seduced by an officer, who was, by the way, married. They had regular sex during his military service, and enjoyed many privileges because of it. He also knew some guys in Banja Luka whom he has sex with occasionally. Besides that he also goes 'man-hunting' in public toilets and in the fortress. When he is free he comes to Belgrade, where he usually spends his time trying to pick someone up at the railway station or the bus depot, and on Ada Island in the summer. During military actions he refrains from raping men so that his companions do not think he is gay. But he makes up for that by getting his captives to remove their clothes when he takes them to bathe in the river. Or he forces a boy to suck his own father's cock or vice versa. There is no end to such monstrous humiliations, tortures and crushing of human dignity.

He wanted me to tell him about my own sexual experiences, so I did. He said it turned him on and that his cock was already hard. I also had an erection while he was telling me about his sexual adventures with an army officer. He asked me what I like to do in sex — I told him I was active, I liked to fuck and to have my cock sucked. I did not want to tell him that I enjoyed 'other things' just as much, not because I wanted to play an exclusive 'macho fucker', but because I did not want to get into risky sex with him, which might be dangerous for me, because, having in mind his promiscuity in the army, he was a potential carrier of AIDS, syphilis or gonorrhea. He said he liked the same thing, to be 'active', like me. Nevertheless, he did not lose his interest in me because of that. He even asked me how long my cock was, which is not typical for someone who is exclusively active. I told him it was big and fat, which made his eyes glow. It was clear that he wasn't as selective as he claimed when it comes to roles in sex. We finally decided to go somewhere and have sex despite our sexual incompatibility. He wasn't very attractive to me, in spite of his strong and manly appearance. He was too 'bulky' for my taste.

Curiosity was my main motive in having sex with him. I wanted to try how it feels to have sex with a mass murderer, a cut-throat and a war criminal. That wish fits in with my 'life philosophy' that you should try everything — in my case 'everything' refers to frequent sexual adventures. I am often the victim of my superficial belief that a successful and happy life consists of a great number of interesting and exciting events, whether pleasant or unpleasant experiences. My search for a meaning in life is itself a reaction to my previous obsession with searching for the hidden meaning and the Absolute outside everyday reality. Disappointed with the unrealised metaphysical meaning, I returned to physical pleasures.

Having all that in mind, I couldn't resist the opportunity to have sex with a war criminal. The wish to be caressed by hands that tortured and killed people was not a reflection of a pathological, morbid sexual fantasy but rather an infantile curiosity to try even that — just to try how it feels. It reminds me of how I made a hole with scissors in a big colourful ball I had been given as a present just to see what was inside. It was a reflection of the mistaken notion that all valuable and essentially important things are hidden somewhere within. However it turned out that the value of the ball lay more in its outer layer than in its hollow inside. It's the same with life but I simply had to have sex with this guy. At that moment I didn't think it was stupid and naive to consider criminals different in sex from others. They are neither better nor worse, neither more passionate nor more gentle than others.

★★★

If we had met under different circumstances, the guy would have probably have killed me. If I was a Muslim or a Croat, he would torture and kill me, and maybe he'd do the same if he knew about my antimilitarist and antinationalist political attitude. On the other hand, if I had any power, I would condemn him to death and have him shot. So we would both be able to kill each other with no mercy under certain circumstances. But now, on the contrary, we were going to bed to make love and caress each other with tenderness. Damned sex, you're capable of doing anything because of it. It is a magnet which draws together people who are incompatible outside the erotic context. This contradictory and absurd situation gave me an additional turn-on.

I took him to Milija's place, because I did not dare take him to my home. I did not want to make love in haste in a park, a doorway or public garage. We walked because I did not want him to see I had a car. When we got there we had to ring the doorbell for a long time because Milija was already in bed. He was in his pyjamas, but he let us in because he obviously liked the look of the guy with me. Then the three of us talked for a bit, Milija asking intrusive questions. In order to cut the unnecessary introduction short and prevent any loss of time, I said we were in a hurry. Milija turned off the lights and went out into the hall leaving the door slightly ajar. The two of us took our clothes off and lay down. We caressed and kissed passionately, pushing our tongues deep into each other's mouths. He had a fabulous body and a big cock — bigger than mine — which was constantly hard. He licked my chest and my belly, hesitating to start the 'real thing'. Perhaps he was ashamed of Milija looking in from the hall. I whispered to him, "Give it a lick." He hesitated but then he grabbed my cock and started sucking it hard.

In the meantime Milija had joined us. He first sucked the guy's cock while we caressed, then put some cream on himself and sat on his cock. They then stood up, Milija bent over the couch and the other fucking him hard, kissing and masturbating me all the time. Milija moaned and groaned while the murderer 'pierced' him with his huge cock. We all came that way, the guy in the old man's arsehole, me in the guy's hand. Milija gave him five million dinars, although he did not ask anything.

Then we dressed and left. He took me to Sat and bought me a coke and a sandwich. Eating our sandwiches on the way, we went to Republic Square as he wanted to see demonstrators and opposition representatives of the Serb Renewal Movement, who were on a hunger strike demanding freedom for Vuk and Danica Drašković. The square was crowded with people, but also with policemen in mufti, who looked at us and scowled. From there, we went to the Astoria Hotel, where he was staying. A colleague of his from Banja Luka was waiting for him there. On the way he jumped over street flower-pots and pavement fences, saying he was in good shape. He said that he was so strong and skilful that he could rob and beat-up at least fifty people a day. At the end of Balkanska Street there sat a dirty drunken whore. She asked him for a cigarette. He said he didn't smoke so we walked on towards the hotel. Then suddenly he had this idea to pick up the whore: "Get her to wash herself then we can fuck her!" I said I wasn't interested, and that I was in a hurry. He, however, decided to go back and pick her up, planning to take her back to his hotel and fuck her, together with his companion. We took leave of each other at that point. I breathed a sigh of relief, got in my car and drove off to the park.

September 15th, 1993

The Iraqi Syndrome

I have been going around supermarkets for days trying to find enough food. There is a shortage of milk, cheese, delicatessen, eggs, biscuits, toothpaste, shampoo, etc. It would be stupid to list all the goods which cannot be found in the shops when almost all goods are unavailable. Shelves in shops are empty, as in the images we use to see on TV programmes about Poland, for instance or the ex-Soviet Union. We had no idea then that we would go through the same situation. Up until recently there was enough food for basic needs although the prices were extremely high so only those with money were able to buy. But now having lots of money isn't very helpful because there's simply nothing in the shops.

Some goods are now distributed by the government. They give us coupons for one litre of oil, one kilogram of salt, detergent and six kilograms of flour per month. Only these things can be bought in shops. Old people say that food supplies were greater even in the Second World War. This government has made Serbia the most miserable and isolated country in the world. Even when sanctions against Yugoslavia are lifted, the economic, cultural and social consequences will last for a long time. It will take us at least ten years to get back to a normal way of life.

The most endangered group are those who have the lowest incomes, most of all retired persons. The irony is that it was these above all who voted for the ruling party and the present government. I cannot but repeat the main motto of the party during the election campaign: 'That's the way it should be!' The sentence has acquired an ironic meaning.

I read in the newspaper that one retired person commits suicide every other day in Belgrade alone. After they voted for 'heavenly Serbia', they seem to be in a hurry to get to heaven as soon as possible. A married couple killed themselves because they were only able to buy a quarter of bread and half a litre of milk a day with their pension. A sixty-year old pensioner had just enough money to buy a bottle of brandy and a litre of gas. First he drank up the brandy, then he used the gas to burn himself to death.

But it's not only pensioners that kill themselves because of the crisis and famine. Twenty-five such cases have been reported since the beginning of the year in the region of Valjevo. A forty-year-old engineer employed in the Krušik factory burned himself to death in a forest not far from his family home having left a message saying that he was fed up with everything. Another man of that age got into his car and drove onto the rails towards a head-on collision with an oncoming train. When will our people stop behaving fatalistically and thinking that whatever happens to them is an act of God? When will people wake up from their docility, submission and suffering?

Our health institutions are also in terrible shape. It is a great misfortune to fall ill. Our medicine has returned to the Middle Ages: nurses use the same needle for several injections; they sterilise surgical gloves which were not meant to be resterilised, so it sometimes happens that the gloves fall apart during operations like rotten pieces of cloth, right on the surgeon's hands; there is no gauze, and even if they are fortunate enough to find some, there are no plasters to stick the gauze to the patient's body. Patients are required to bring with them everything they need for being hospitalised, treated or operated on (needles, anaesthetics, gauze, plasters, scalpels, syringes, medicines, etc.). If any of these things are in fact available they are only to be found in privately owned pharmacies where the prices are astronomical. Most people on average incomes cannot afford these things. With all this in mind doctors say that we are going through the 'Iraqi syndrome' — there won't be any sick or elderly people soon because they will all die.

City transport is also in a disastrous state. There is no gas or oil, so traffic is reduced. People wait for hours in order to catch a bus and travel from one part to another. There is a shortage of tyres and spare parts and most vehicles are old and non-functional. Breakdowns and accidents happen frequently. It recently became literally dangerous to travel on city buses. One bus had a flat tyre or the so-called air pillow exploded making a large hole in the floor of the bus through which a woman fell; one of the wheels ran over her and killed her. I always bear this in mind whenever I am able to board a bus.

This city has become an extremely dangerous place in which to live. Criminals, both the unimportant ones and those organised ones who collaborate with politicians, rule in all segments of society. Cars are frequently stolen, apartments broken into, refugees occupy other people's flats illegally, there are frequent assaults on the streets — necklaces and purses are grabbed away from women. Thieves raid people's apartments wearing stockings over their heads even when people are at home. They ask the occupants to show them where they keep their money and valuables, threatening them with guns and knives. Sometimes the thieves wear police or postman's uniforms and when their victims open their doors they dash in threatening them and then run off with the valuables. (This in fact happened to a friend of mine quite recently).

A gang of bandits entered through a window the house of a man who'd placed an advert in a local newspaper trying to sell some wooden building materials — they cut his throat and stole his money. Thieves broke into my neighbour's flat through a window whilst he was away and stole everything. I installed iron bars on my windows and more bars on my door because of such insecurity. The mentality of a 'besieged fortress' prevails everywhere. People purchase special imported locks, put extra locks on their doors, install bars, and those who can afford it install burglar alarm systems and armoured doors. I lock the steering wheel in my car with a hook in addition to having a car alarm and disconnect the wire between the ignition coil and the distributor head during the night. In spite of such precautions, my windshield wipers were stolen — the alarm did not go off. I installed special anti-robbery screws on the wheels, but already one wheel has been removed. Nothing is safe anymore.

Belgrade is being demolished, degraded and crowded with boors. A large number of refugees from Bosnia contribute to the general deterioration. They moved directly from 'their' mountains and villages to the centre of the city, to Prince Mihaijlo Street. You can hear their southern Bosnian accent everywhere. and can not avoid their crude primitive faces. They sell foreign money in street all over town shouting: "Foreign money! Foreign money!" Moskva restaurant is crowded with them, so the decent people who used to frequent the place no longer go there — including young couples, students, elderly people and gays. They no longer go partly because of these refugees and partly because of the high prices. The only group who can afford the prices now are the dealers from Bosnia.

Money 'dealers' also go to Staklenac to have a drink or to use the toilets. They have noticed that gays frequent the place so they often attack and beat them up. The other day I noticed blood stains in the toilets. Before that I'd heard they'd caught a boy there and bashed his head against a concrete wall, they then knocked him down and put the boot in. There are also more and more stray dogs roaming about, which makes Belgrade seem provincial. The dogs are skinny and covered in scabs whereas before the dogs were plump and sleek. Now they remind me of the mangy creatures without stomachs I saw in India, Egypt and Thailand. They root around trash containers and garbage cans looking for edible rubbish. There are a number of cases of these packs of strays attacking isolated passers-by.

The streets are now empty by eleven at night. People do not have enough gas to drive their own cars and city buses are increasingly rare. In the evening the city looks like a ghost-town — there are no cars, no casual strollers. People are locking themselves in their own homes and watching TV — which in turn contaminates their minds with nationalist propaganda. According to the prevailing, generally accepted theory of 'the international conspiracy', Western countries led by the United States and Germany are to blame for all our problems, along with the Vatican and the Islamic countries. The whole world is wrong and only this regime is right!

September 30th, 1993

Lost Confidence in Men

A local Belgrade magazine, *Metro* — dealing with problems of public transport and hygiene in the city — contains an article about the situation in public toilets. Like a similar article in *Politika* a couple of years ago this pinpoints the main problem as homosexuals. The woman journalist visited several public toilets and wrote her report based on the statements of several cleaning women, most of whom are illiterate Gypsies. They said that the worst place to work in is the toilets in the underground passage in front of the Albanija Building, in other words Staklenac. A great number of homosexuals can be found there, according to the article, though it is true that they never disturb the cleaning ladies. When other toilet users complain, the cleaners are too afraid to do anything about it. They maintained that the situation was a lot better when the place was crowded with smugglers selling foreign money; because they couldn't stand the sight of so many homosexuals, they simply 'cleansed' the place of them. The journalist quotes two statements by cleaning ladies who wanted to stay anonymous:

"People can't imagine how many homosexuals there are in this city. It seems to me that every second man in this city is a faggot. There are various kinds of them, from young ones to old, and it often happens that the old ones seduce the younger ones. I once recognised a gynaecologist from the clinic in Narodnog Fronta Street, and caught him performing his homosexual activities in the toilet near Albanija. I was shocked when I even recognised a priest, who of course was not wearing his robes at the time. There are many young homosexuals. Older people are usually nicely dressed, so you'd never guess that they were homosexuals if you met them in the street."

"They meet here, and this place is known for that. Homosexuals often ask for money for their 'services'. They don't do what they do inside the booths, but right in front of the urinals, so that they can be seen by everyone who uses the toilet. There are some boys of twelve or thirteen who come here to watch such things, then they do the same... A reporter should come here with a camera to take pictures of what is going on here. It's terrible... You won't believe it but there are many retired men among homosexuals. It happened to me once, while I was sweeping the floor of a booth, that a man stood behind me, dropped his trousers and did that thing which I'm decent enough not to name. Fortunately I knew such men were cowards so I ran after him with a wooden stick. There are people from all walks of life, from the poor to doctors and politicians. Imagine, there are people who have normal family lives and who come here to do things with homosexuals. I've seen everything since I took this job! I've lost all my confidence in men!"

After reading such things I don't know whether to laugh or cry. It is tragic to see both the journalist and the cleaning ladies so cheerful about the 'homo-cleansing' of the toilets. They didn't mention that it was done with metal bars, knocking them down to the ground and kicking them, hitting heads against walls, etc. and that the police did nothing whatsoever. On the other hand, some of the stupid things and the ridiculous prejudices voiced by the cleaners are really funny. The article is yet another example of the serio-comic silly things which are said about gays in our media.

October 29th, 1993

Death to the Circumcised

This afternoon I met Branko at Staklenac, a Bosnian guy whom I'd had sex with about ten years ago in Sarajevo. Now he lives with his wife and two children in a refugee hostel in Belgrade. He looks quite old and wrinkled now, so he seems much older than me, although he's actually younger. We often see each other in cruising places but I avoid talking to him because he's a bit of a bore, you can never shake him off once he starts talking. He stopped me to tell me something quite interesting.

First he told me that he'd seen a bunch of hoodlums cruelly beating a gay person in Karadjordje Park yesterday. He'd tried to run off into the street but they chased after him, knocked him down on the pavement, beat him, kicked him and tore his clothes. They shouted, "Faggot! Wanna get fucked up the arse? Take this!" The poor guy lay in the street all bloody with his clothes ripped. When his attackers left he could hardly limp home or to the hospital. Hoodlums are becoming increasingly dangerous and violent in that park. They attack in groups using not only their feet and fists but also chains, metal bars and similar objects. A young lad was so beaten up with metal bars that he lay in a a coma for days on the brink of death. He lay in hospital for months before his life was finally saved. An article in *Politika* dealt with the case, illustrating a wider problem of the increase in crimes of violence in Belgrade. I've also heard that hoodlums beat up a guy named Dragan so badly that he'll have to spend the rest of his life confined to a wheelchair. The culprits have yet to be traced.

However, the Bosnian guy didn't stop me just to talk about the increase of violence in the park but about something else even more dramatic. About ten days previously he was at the Army Hospital, to visit his relative who'd been wounded somewhere in Bosnia. The next bed was occupied by another wounded soldier from Bosnia. He was being visited by his brother, a tall short-haired fellow with a manly appearance. They made contact because they'd had similar roots and fates and as it so happened they were from the same part of Bosnia. They went somewhere for a drink where they began chatting. It turned out that the macho hunk was also fond of men. They went to his room at the Hotel Slavija where they had wild sex. The guy was extremely well-built and had a really big cock which was hard as a rock. After Branko had given him a blow job and the guy had fucked him, they lay down to have a rest and a smoke. Branko noticed that the expression on his lover's face suddenly changed. He felt something was coming up. The guy took out a gun he'd concealed under his pillow and put the cold metal against Branko's forehead saying:

"You motherfucker! I kill guys like you in Bosnia!"

"Guys like what?" Poor Branko could hardly speak.

"Muslims! What d'you think you are?"

"But -- I'm not a Muslim, I'm a Serb!"

"Don't lie to me, you scum! I'm not that stupid. You're circumcised!"

The bloke really thought Branko was a Muslim when he saw he was circumcised, and he found it a good enough reason to kill him. Branko somehow managed to convince the guy he was not a Muslim and that he was circumcised because he'd had phimosis. He showed him his refugee documents, even a photo of his wife and kids. I just wonder what would have happened if he hadn't managed to convince him, and if he really had been Muslim, since there are several Muslims in Belgrade gay circles. Lastly he could have been a Jew or even a circumcised American.

I remembered something so I asked Branko to tell me just where that loony was from.

"From Banja Luka."

"And what was his name?"

"Mirko."

"Mirko? A tall, short-haired guy? A member of a sort of special commando force?"

"Yes."

"Jesus, I know him! I met him at the railway station on July 5th this year. I'll never forget my encounter with him. He told me so many terrible things. He showed me the papers of a Croat whose throat he'd cut and told me the story of a Muslim soldier he'd tied to a tree with a piece of wire and then cut him up with a welding torch!"

"Yeah! That's him alright. He told me he that if his brother died he'd go on a cruel revenge mission against Muslims. Meanwhile his brother has actually died!"

"So far, he's done so many horrible things, torturing and killing people in cold blood. God knows what other things he'll do now after his brother's death!"

"Did you have sex with him?" he asked me curiously.

"Why yes, he gave me a blow job."

While we were talking a handsome blond guy came in. I interrupted our conversation and went after the guy into the toilets. It was a false alarm as the guy was completely uninterested. He just took a leak and left. The circumcised Bosnian had also left when I came out.

December 31st, 1993

The End of History

Fukuyama's theory of the end of history is 'in' these days. As the critics say, the idea is neither new nor right, but it is any case provocative and actual after the fall of communism. According to the author, the present time is not just the end of the Cold War, but also the final point of the ideological evolution of mankind and of the global spread of Western liberal democracy as the supreme form of human organisation. This of course does not suggest the end of events, but the end in the evolution of human thinking on primary principles. Does that mean there will be no new ideas, utopias of a social system better than the existing liberal democracy? I'm inclined to believe in this theory. The rest of history may just bring slightly different variations.

Inspired by this theory I intended to announce the end of my own history. Rereading the pages of my diary I conclude that events, thoughts and emotions I go through recur in more or less the same forms. I do the same things every day, always lamenting about being lonely and the feeling of meaninglessness, trying to reach self-oblivion in sex and so forth. Tiring. Boring. Hopeless. Since my life has repeated itself in the last few years, always making the same circles, I can't see any possibility that anything will change essentially before the end of my life. It has entered the final ideological phase after which there is no evolution and no change. In spite of everything I hope to live longer. I do not want to anticipate my biological death. There will be more events and falling on evil days, but they will be replicas of the past, bad copies of past events. There will be nothing new in my life. Unlike Fukuyama's theory where the end means an ideal state, the state where my individuality stops is far from ideal. It is a state characterised by failure in my striving to create an 'ideal self' and lying on the bottom where I have landed up after trying to reach the top. Now I'm lying down here without the ability to move, waiting for the end. I'm disposing of all my intellectual aspirations and devoting myself to sex and hedonism. Freud's impulsive id has gained a victory inside me.

Having all that in mind, it is logical that there is no point in my keeping a diary any longer. There is no point in recording events and feelings which repeat themselves. The whole diary could be reduced to several key words such as sex, loneliness, depression, obsession with myself, etc. It is time for me to stop the history of my life because it, the history, has come to its end.